ALSO BY MAGGIE & NIGEL PERCY

The Busy Person's Guide To Energy Clearing

The Busy Person's Guide To Space Clearing

The Busy Person's Guide To Ghosts, Curses & Aliens

The Busy Person's Guide: The Complete Series on Energy Clearing

The Nature of Intuition: Understand & Harness Your Intuitive Ability

Caring For Your Animal Companion: The Intuitive, Natural Way To A Happy, Healthy Pet

Space Clearing: Beyond Feng Shui

Ask The Right Question: The Essential Sourcebook of Good Dowsing Questions

Dowsing Ethics: Replacing Intentions With Integrity

The Practical Pendulum Series, Volumes 1-4

Pendulum Proficiency: You Can Learn To Dowse

How To Dowse Accurately & With Confidence

Dowsing Pitfalls & Protection

Dowse Your Way To Health: An Introduction To Health Dowsing

Dowsing: Practical Enlightenment

101 Amazing Things You Can Do With Dowsing

The Dowsing State: Secret Key To Accurate Dowsing

The Dowsing Encyclopedia

The Essence Of Dowsing by Nigel Percy

The Credibility Of Dowsing, edited by Nigel Percy

Healing Made Simple: Change Your Mind & Improve Your Health

Dowsing Box Set

Dowsing Reference Library

DOWSING FOR HEALTH

AWAKEN YOUR HIDDEN TALENT

MAGGIE PERCY
NIGEL PERCY

Copyright © 2018 Maggie and Nigel Percy

ISBN: 978-1-946014-27-6 (Ebook version)

ISBN: 978-1-946014-28-3 (Paperback version)

All rights reserved. No part of this publication may be reproduced, distributed or transmitted in any form or by any means, including photocopying, recording, or other electronic or mechanical methods, without the prior written permission of the publisher, except in the case of brief quotations embodied in critical reviews and certain other noncommercial uses permitted by copyright law. For permission requests, write to the publisher, addressed "Attention: Permissions Coordinator," at the address below.

Maggie Percy

150 Buck Run E

Dahlonega, GA 30533

Email: discoveringdowsing@gmail.com

Natural forces within us are the true healers of disease

-Hippocrates

CONTENTS

Preface — ix
Acknowledgments — xiii
Getting The Most Out Of This Book — xv
Warning — xix

1. What Is Health Dowsing? — 1
2. Using Dowsing Effectively For Your Health — 23
3. What Is Health? — 30
4. Major Factors That Affect Health — 47
5. Dowsing Accurately — 66
6. Dowsing Techniques — 74
7. Dowsing Protocols — 81
8. Dowsing For Yourself — 162
9. Dowsing For Others — 179
10. Pitfalls — 188
11. The Healing Process — 199
12. Going Beyond — 212
13. Bonus: Questions From "Ask The Right Question" — 222
14. Resources — 263

Please Leave A Review — 267
About The Authors — 269

PREFACE

This book is not an encyclopedia of common dis-eases with a list of remedies. You can search the internet for information on dis-eases and natural and conventional solutions for them, so there is no need to repeat that here.

Instead, this book will help you develop expertise in health dowsing —getting answers about your health that your rational mind cannot give you—but to us, that is just one step in creating optimal health, so this book also helps you build a solid foundation in understanding what health is to you, how to create your health goals and what factors affect your health, as well as teaching you approaches to building a health regimen. After all, you are unique, and one of the biggest benefits of health dowsing is that it allows you to address your unique health issues and goals, instead of giving you a one-size-fits-all answer to everything.

We give you a brief refresher on key dowsing techniques for health dowsing and an extensive group of health dowsing protocols that will help you unravel the causes of health problems and reveal the most effective, safe treatments for you. Included are dowsing protocols for evaluating health as a preventive measure and ways to use dowsing to create the optimal health program for your goals. We also cover dowsing for yourself and dowsing for others and point out common pitfalls and how to remedy or avoid them.

Lastly, we touch on the idea that by creating a clear picture of what health is to you and focusing your intention on creating it, you will see unexpected side benefits from mastering health dowsing, from developing your intuition to becoming more empowered.

As you may guess from the breadth and depth of this material, one does not become an expert health dowser overnight. Indeed, as a dowser, you are always growing and learning. That is because dowsing is not a psychic or magical activity, but a natural human skill that requires training and practice. The more you use health dowsing, the more your skill will grow.

In this book, we draw on our many years of experience and share with you methods that have worked for us and saved us untold dollars, wasted effort and heartache. Health dowsing has given us miraculous results, but one doesn't become healthy overnight; in fact, it is not desirable to attain perfect health overnight. Healing is a journey, and this book is meant to be a tool for your health journey.

Healing is personal. Your path will be unique. Your viewpoint may not be the same as ours. We have found our view of health has changed over the years, and we encourage you to maintain an open mind as you seek health, because in spite of what Science says, it has only discovered a small percent of the knowledge required to help you be healthy mentally, physically and energetically. Even if you have learned everything Science has to share, your rational mind does not have all the facts, and that is where dowsing comes in. There is just so much to learn.

Health dowsing is practical. It can save you time, effort and money, not to mention heartbreak. But it is also an amazingly empowering, enlightening activity that can potentially change your whole life for the better in ways you can't imagine at the start of the journey.

We don't claim to know everything about dowsing and health, but we have accumulated a lot of experience, and this book shares everything we've learned with you so that your path to mastery and success can be smoother and easier than ours.

Maggie Percy

January 20, 2018

ACKNOWLEDGMENTS

Every book is the result of a group effort. This book could not have been written without a great deal of help from my husband Nigel, who is an expert health dowser and my alpha reader and editor.

Thanks to the members of the Dowsing Tribe who took the time to answer my survey in the months before I began to write this book. Their input helped guide me to include material that I otherwise may have neglected to cover, making the book more complete and useful.

I am indebted to the advance readers who helped us launch the book and provided reviews and valuable comments.

And finally, we are grateful to all our readers, dowsers who, like us, see the amazing potential of dowsing for helping to create optimal health and longevity.

GETTING THE MOST OUT OF THIS BOOK

You've bought this book because you're eager to learn the practice of health dowsing. You probably have a health challenge, or you want to add dowsing as a tool for creating the best health possible. Maybe you even want to do health dowsing professionally. Congratulations! This book will help you achieve your goals, whatever they are.

But don't be too eager to dive right into the actual dowsing, because health dowsing is a complex topic, and we want to prepare you to get the best results, which means we must be sure we are all starting from the same point.

We first need to discuss what health dowsing is, and what it is not, so that you don't become confused with the content we present later. Furthermore, you probably have some questions about how you can best use health dowsing for optimal results, or you may question if you are prepared to dowse for health, so we'll give you guidance there. It's also vital that we get you thinking about what exactly health is to you, because it isn't the same thing to everyone. We're going to teach you how to make health goals and to be aware of key elements that impact health, so that we can later talk about using dowsing to gather information you'll need for creating optimal health. We have a chapter on the most important aspects of dowsing technique, and then we cover dowsing techniques you will need for health dowsing.

In summary, health dowsing is a tool, and just showing you how to use the tool is nice, but if you want to craft excellent health, then you need to understand how to approach health for the best results. In this book, we endeavor to give you a 'big picture' outlook as well as teach you the nitty gritty of health dowsing, so that you can fine tune it to your unique needs and get the most out of it.

As with any skill, health dowsing takes time to master. To become a skilled athlete, you need to build a strong, flexible body before you dive into the particulars of your sport. To become a good pianist, you must practice many drills that make your hands flexible, and you must learn to read music. Becoming skilled at anything takes time and practice, and dowsing is no exception; you can't just jump to the advanced part. Be patient with yourself.

You may feel you are a veteran dowser because you've been dowsing for years, and perhaps you are correct. But our experience has shown that most dowsers, even if they dowse often, only dowse for a couple things. They don't use dowsing widely in their everyday life. While you have a head start on most people if you know how to dowse and have been using it off and on for years, you will probably benefit from putting your pendulum aside briefly and stepping back and thinking about health in a broader sense before you dive into the actual dowsing. It takes us years to create health issues, and resolving them usually takes time, too, so we advise you to be patient and try to adopt a whole new way of looking at health, because a new perspective is your most powerful tool for change.

You could skip the first chapters and dive right into the section on dowsing protocols, but you will do yourself a disservice if you take short cuts. We want to give you a solid foundation on which to build your health dowsing, and we urge you to be patient and go through each chapter, doing any exercises, because if you do that, you will be far more likely to reap the greatest benefits from health dowsing.

You are unique, and we often mention that in this book and encourage you to think and formulate your own personal goals, which is one reason we have a lot of content to help you step back and think about health in general, so you can find the best approach for you.

We aren't here to tell you your life's purpose or the one true path to health; that is unique for each person, and you are the best person to discover those things. Our mission is to help you learn to use dowsing to discover your path to wellness and to enjoy a healthy life with optimal longevity.

Finally, what we share here are methods and outlooks that have given us success over our many years of personal and professional health dowsing. Like most experts, we have opinions about the best way to do what we do, so be prepared to hear strong opinions. It's OK if you disagree with them, but if so, please think carefully about why that is, rather than emotionally rejecting what we say. You are entitled to your beliefs and opinions; just make sure they are helping you reach your goals. We have found over time that it is necessary to drop beliefs and attitudes in order to grow and reach our goals. Don't be afraid to do that when it is necessary or desirable.

We have worked hard to acquire our knowledge, but we won't keep any secrets or try to make dowsing seem mysterious or esoteric. We aren't going to make you jump through hoops or 'earn' anything. You will have to invest time and effort, but how much is your choice. We intend to make this knowledge accessible to anyone who is willing to work. We want you to make faster progress in your journey than we did in ours, and we are happy to share so that you can become a successful health dowser.

Take your time and read the entire book from cover to cover. Think about what you have read, and feel free to contact us through any of our websites if you have questions. Happy Dowsing!

WARNING

Congratulations for your interest in using dowsing for health! Before we dive into the material, a warning is required. Please read this carefully and take it seriously.

This book is not a course in dowsing. If you wish to be an accurate health dowser and reap full benefits, you first need to be a masterful dowser. That takes time, training and practice. We urge you to master basic dowsing technique before trying anything as complex as health dowsing. **We consider proper dowsing technique and accuracy a prerequisite for using the material in this book to advantage.**

We also consider it highly valuable for you to have at least one or two healing/energy transformation modalities that you have been trained in and feel confident with, so that you can go beyond just asking questions about your health.

The methods in this book are NOT intended to replace your health care professional. We all need outside help from time to time. The goal of this material is to help you to become empowered to work with your doctor or other health care provider in a more effective and informed way, so that you get better results and save time, effort and money. After all, you are the person who has the most to gain or lose from your health choices, so it makes sense that you have an active role in shaping your health.

We trust you to seek outside help if you have a physical or mental/emotional condition that you cannot resolve easily or quickly. We also urge you to always get a second and even a third opinion before taking action on the results of your health dowsing.

The goal of this book is to empower you to participate in your own health program. It is not designed to fully prepare you to become a professional health dowser, as laws vary. We urge you to get good advice if you decide you want to use health dowsing professionally. There is much more to it than just being a good health dowser; you need to know the law.

Do not under any circumstance use any methods in this book for anyone outside your immediate family without consulting the law that applies to your country and locality. You are entitled to care for your health and that of your immediate family (at least at the time of this writing), but before offering to help anyone else, you must consult your local, regional and national laws regarding health care to make sure you are within legal bounds.

1
WHAT IS HEALTH DOWSING?

We have a zillion dramatic stories that prove the value of health dowsing, but this personal one is probably our favorite.

Some years ago, when Nigel was dressing, I noticed a mole on his back. Nigel has lots of moles, so that wasn't what grabbed my attention. It was the change in the mole—its size, color and border—that concerned me. I'd studied a photographic brochure from the dermatologist years before, because living in the desert and having an Irish complexion prompted me to be vigilant. This mole alarmed me. I became more concerned when he told me it had recently started to itch.

Because we are health dowsers, we didn't rush right to the doctor. While the symptoms were alarming, it wasn't 100% clear that we needed a doctor, but yet, it wasn't obvious that we could dismiss it. So we used our dowsing protocol to figure out what to do. Our dowsing indicated we shouldn't go to the doctor, and that we could treat it successfully at home. So we did.

After about two weeks of daily dowsing and applying remedies, Nigel's mole fell off in the shower, leaving a perfect, smooth layer of skin underneath.

We can't claim that the mole was precancerous or cancerous and was cured, but that is not the point. Based on the outcome, it is obvious we didn't need a doctor (someone else might need a doctor in the same situation, which is why dowsing is a vital tool). Health dowsing saved us time, trouble and perhaps a negative outcome, as you will see in the details below.

Being dowsers, we don't immediately rush to the doctor or vet with health concerns. We make sure consulting a doctor is the best route to health, that it's necessary and will benefit us. Obviously, if you have a terrible cut or a compound fracture, you don't need to dowse what to do. Likewise, if you have a slight headache or cold, you can just self-medicate with whatever remedy works for you. It's the in-between cases, the not-horrible, not-minor ones that bedevil you.

If you don't dowse, your action is based on your fears, biases or habits. You may go to a doctor out of fear, or you may choose not to go to a vet because of money. Your results are far from guaranteed in such situations, because **you are simply guessing**. And you are allowing your prejudices to direct you, rather than taking informed action.

How often have you spent a ton of time and money on a perceived health issue that the doctor or vet couldn't fix? Most of our consultation clients had stories like that. One claimed to have invested $100,000 over a period of years unsuccessfully trying to find an answer to her health issue. On the other hand, how many times have you failed to seek professional help at first, maybe because of money problems, and later discovered time was of the essence, and you lost a chance for healing? Hopefully this will never happen to you.

As a health dowser, you can make the right choice far more often in gray-area cases. Nothing is 100%, but your accuracy for choosing well is improved significantly with dowsing. That is because instead of acting from fear or prejudice or habit (guessing), you focus your intuition on your health goals and how to best achieve them. You are in effect taking charge of your healing process.

Here are the steps in the sequence we use in situations like this, with the answers we got during the mole incident.

Warning: Note that we had two masterful dowsers with years of experience both dowsing the same questions. We do NOT recommend you make important health decisions based solely on your own dowsing. Get a second and even a third opinion from a dowser you trust.

Step 1: Goals

We had previously set our personal goals for health, and for when we wanted to get a 'yes' response about seeking outside help. You are unique. Your goals will be shaped by your finances, your values and your personal desires. For example, we haven't always had much disposable income, but we have between us a good bit of experience in healing methods and biology. We are therefore more confident about self-work than some people would be. You need to set goals that suit you. See the section on 'Setting Health Goals' in the 'What Is Health?' chapter for details.

This step is best settled at leisure when you have no health challenges, so that you can approach it in a relaxed manner and take the time to think things out, write them down and sleep on them.

Step 2: Level In Effects Of Process

The first question we always ask when we get a physical symptom is what is the overall level in effects on our long term health and well-being of whatever process is causing this symptom. This acknowledges that not all pain is 'bad' and that a symptom is not a cause. We are not interested in treating symptoms. We want to heal root causes.

For example, if you start an exercise program, the muscle pain is a good thing in the long run, because it is a sign of you becoming stronger, though unpleasant in the present. If you assume it's bad simply because you hurt, you would quit your exercise program.

So if you dowsed about the long term level in effects on you of whatever is causing the muscle pain, you'd get a positive number, because in the long run, the process of becoming more fit is good for you. We use a +10 to -10 scale, with 0 being neutral. Negative numbers indicate a dis-ease process. See the 'Level In Effects' section in the 'Dowsing Techniques' chapter for details on how to master this simple but critical dowsing question. The actual dowsing protocol may be found in the 'Is It Good Or Bad?' section in the 'Dowsing Protocols' chapter.

We got a high positive number in the case of Nigel's mole for the long term effect on his health. Not what you would expect from the appearance of it, is it? That number told us the overall process was beneficial for him, no matter how scary the mole appeared.

Step 3: Consulting A Doctor

We then used the same scale, +10 to -10, and asked the overall level in effects on Nigel's health of consulting a doctor about this symptom. We got a -8, which suggests a very negative outcome if we consulted a doctor. You would only want to consider going to a professional if the number was positive. Why spend time and money if it is 0 or less? In addition, a -8 would suggest that you would end up in worse shape than if you did nothing.

We often wondered if doing a biopsy on the mole or allowing a doctor to speak his beliefs would have caused a bad outcome. In other words, it isn't always good or neutral to get professional assistance. In some cases it can be harmful to your health. An example would be of someone who is allergic to the dye used in certain imaging tests. What might be a good path for one person could lead to death for another.

The 'Do You Need A Doctor?' section in the 'Dowsing Protocols' chapter goes into detail on this question, which is one of the most valuable dowsing questions you can master. If we had gotten a positive number, especially a +8 or higher, we would have made an appointment. A low positive number might have stimulated us to ask some more questions to see why it was only mildly positive to go to a doctor.

Step 4: Self-Care

Even if you get a positive number for seeing a doctor, you can follow up after the appointment with dowsing what you can do to help facilitate healing. In this case, we got a clear "don't go to a doctor," so we then asked if there was anything we could do to help make the healing process smoother, faster or safer. The 'Dowsing Techniques' chapter discusses this.

We got a 'yes' and also got a 'yes' when we asked if the method was known to us. We then dowsed a list of our methods and applied the one that tested best.

For us, methods include essential oils, herbs, tapping, symbols, colors, statement of intent and a variety of other tools and healing methods we are familiar with. You will benefit from learning the use of several simple methods so that you can turn to them in situations like this.

Step 6: Repeat As Needed

We went through this process from Step 3 onward every single day to acknowledge that things can change. We were open to going to a doctor at any point, but it never tested better than -8. We found we had to use a different healing method each day on the mole, but the entire dowsing process took no more than a couple minutes, and the remedies were simple.

While this process may sound complex to you if you haven't used it, it is truly fast once you learn it. Over the years, we have used this procedure countless times for ourselves and our pets. I have been surprised at the number of times dowsing indicated we didn't need a doctor or vet. In 100% of those cases, the outcome was positive when we followed our dowsing. Considering that a visit to the vet can cost hundreds of dollars and the time spent in waiting rooms and travel to and from doctor's offices, it's no shock to realize we have saved thousands of dollars and a lot of time by being able to dowse health questions. It is also possible that by following our dowsing, we avoided very negative outcomes in some cases.

Dowsing for health is a priceless tool. The goal of this book is to help you learn how to dowse for health issues and vastly improve the results you get over when you simply guess what to do in those in-between situations.

What Is Health Dowsing?

It's important to start this book with a clear definition of what health dowsing is, because there is some confusion not only about what health dowsing is, but what dowsing itself is. So before we plunge into the subject of dowsing for health, let's set the stage for what is to come by defining terms.

Dowsing is a natural human skill, not a psychic ability. Everyone is intuitive to some extent, and everyone has intuitive senses. While modern culture does not acknowledge or train you in the use of those senses, you have the latent ability to use them. What is dowsing? Dowsing is a way to tap into your natural intuitive sensing array on demand to get answers to questions your rational mind cannot answer.

Your rational mind is trained for many years in school, but your intuitive sensing is ignored or laughed at. As a result, your intuition may not be strongly developed. You may not use it, and you may not trust it. Like a person who has no muscles, you aren't comfortable or competent exercising something you've never tried to develop. If you learn proper dowsing technique and practice, you can become a confident, accurate dowser.

Health dowsing is using dowsing to get answers to your health questions, and it is a tool to help you build a health program or take right action to create the health you want. While health dowsing is not a healing method, it combines well with any healing method. Health dowsing does not transform energies; it answers questions. But it combines well with energy transformation and healing techniques.

If health dowsing isn't a healing method, why do nearly 1 out of every 3 dowsers surveyed in 2018 believe that it is? The close working relationship between health dowsing and healing methods is probably the cause of confusion about what health dowsing is. We can't be sure exactly how and when health dowsing, as an application of dowsing, became perceived as a healing modality. Back in the 90s, when we first learned to dowse, it was pretty clear that dowsing was asking questions and getting answers. But even then, it was obvious that health dowsing was the most popular application, so a lot of people started using dowsing for health.

There were few courses and almost no books on the subject at that time, and those who taught health dowsing came from varied backgrounds. Most of them were trained in one or more healing methods. Quite a few were fond of using simple statements of intention to transform energies. Some were masterful dowsers, while others were not.

Then (as now), the steps you might see a health dowser take were:

1. Focus on a goal and formulate a good dowsing question to get useful information for solving a health challenge
2. Dowse the question and get the answer
3. Apply a fix to address the issue
4. Check using dowsing to see if the fix worked.

Here's a simple example: A health dowser discovers via dowsing that the cause of your symptom is a noxious line of energy you have been sleeping in. She uses a statement of intention to transform the energy of the line to beneficial. While the energy clears, she spins her pendulum in a neutral swing and asks to be shown a 'yes' when the clearing is complete, or she asks if the clearing has been successful for her goals.

Is it possible that as an observer of this process, you might think that dowsing is not only getting answers, but transforming energies? Can it be that by using a pendulum and having the observer focus on that, the dowser unintentionally leads the observer to think pendulum dowsing is a transformational method rather than just an indicator of when the clearing is done? Or that the pendulum is somehow doing the work?

It would seem logical that if the dowser stopped after getting the dowsing answer that a negative line was at fault and explained what had been discovered and talked about the various options for transforming the energy, it would be clear to the observer that dowsing was not an energy transformation technique. There are many ways to transform a negative line. A statement of intention is one, but you can also use crystals, symbols, fragrance and pegs, among other things. If the dowser had taken the time to discuss and use one of those methods, it would be clear that dowsing ended with the information about the negative line, and another method took over from there. She probably wouldn't have even been able to use the pendulum during the clearing if she were using physical things like crystals to 'anchor' her intention. Even if she used her pendulum to measure how long the clearing took, you would be aware that she was dowsing a question: is the clearing done? You would never form the misconception that crystal healing was a form of dowsing.

The challenge in the above process is that intention, unlike other transformational and healing methods, is invisible. A vitamin, herb, crystal or tone would obviously not be dowsing. Reiki or Jin Shin

Jyutsu are healing methods, and observers would not call them dowsing. But intention alone in the form of a statement is so invisible that it could easily appear to be part of the dowsing process, especially if the dowser measured the time it took to complete the clearing by using a pendulum.

Pendulums have become associated with health dowsing to such an extent that people forget that they are used for many things other than dowsing, like putting people into a hypnotic trance. Just because someone is swinging a pendulum does not mean they are dowsing. More importantly, a pendulum isn't even a requirement for dowsing. The exact same process could take place without a tool.

While this is one explanation for how the confusion started about what health dowsing is, it doesn't explain how widespread the misconception became. Wouldn't you think that if all professionals promoted dowsing as a way of getting answers, the confusion would disappear? The answer is yes. Unfortunately, in any new field you can get many people promoting something, and not all of them use the same definitions or have the same agenda or even the same ethics. For example, herbal extracts have long been used for healing, yet when they were popular in the 19th century, there were plenty of charlatans making money from elixirs that had no value at all. They were called 'snake oil salesmen.'

In dowsing, there are probably very few charlatans, but there were misguided individuals who eagerly promoted dowsing as a healing method because it was so easy to make a statement of intention and swing a pendulum that the original misunderstanding spread virally. A statement of intention is much easier than learning Reiki, Jin Shin Jyutsu, tapping or how to use crystals.

We live in a society that demands instant gratification, and somehow, enough people promoted using a pendulum as a healing method that it caught on. We are grateful that honest practitioners are now calling this method 'pendulum healing' to differentiate it from dowsing. Another easy way to tell the difference between dowsing and pendulum healing is that pendulum healing requires a pendulum; dowsing does not.

We have stuck to the original definition of dowsing and maintain that using intention, while it is appropriate in many cases and can be very powerful, is a separate skill from dowsing. Therefore, if you want to use intention for healing or energy transformation, you need to master the skill of using intention, just like you need to master any healing method, because it does require mastery, just as accurate dowsing does.

You will often see a statement of intention called a prayer of intention. This is not a misnomer. Prayer is a statement of intention. And intention can work every bit as well as prayer, which is to say, not at all. If prayer worked consistently, everyone would be praying, wouldn't they? Statements of intention can work, but it requires training and practice for most people to master that skill. Just because some guru says he can change energies with a statement of intention does not mean you can, too.

Don't be dismayed if you misunderstood health dowsing. Health dowsing is actually MORE valuable than any single healing method. Why? Because no healing method works all the time. In fact, most don't give dramatic results in a majority of cases. That's why there are so many healing methods. The trick is to master a few healing methods—one of them can be intention—and use them in your dowsing program.

We have been certified in Spiritual Response Therapy (SRT), Senzar Clearing, Emotional Freedom Technique (EFT), Reiki, Spiritual Healing and Jin Shin Jyutsu for healing and transformation of energies. In addition, we are self-taught in the use of crystals, symbols, sound, fragrance, flower essences, essential oils, herbs and natural remedies. We believe that the more tools you have in your kit, the more you learn and the more successfully you can address a wide variety of challenges.

If we break down the health dowsing process mentioned above and look more closely at it, you will see that dowsing is one thing, and healing/transformation of energy is another. Here are the steps, seen in more detail:

1. Focus on a goal and formulate a good dowsing question to get useful information for solving a health challenge (dowsing)
2. Dowse the question and get the answer (dowsing)
3. Dowse what the best method is for healing or transforming the energies (dowsing)
4. Apply the chosen fix for resolving the problem (healing or energy transformation)
5. Use dowsing to measure success (dowsing)

Step 3 is overlooked by many folks, who just jump to a statement of intention for their 'fix'. But what if a statement of intention isn't going to work? If you don't dowse to find the right method, you can easily pick a poor one. Intention alone rarely works for complex problems, although we do teach people to use it in certain situations.

If you observed a health dowser doing the above steps, and the person dowsed that a statement of intention was the best way to clear the energy, would you understand that the clearing was done by intention, not dowsing? Hopefully, it would be more obvious this way. We think that too many people think intention always works, and they don't have a lot of tools in their kit, so they go straight to intention without considering any other method, but they haven't dowsed that a statement of intention is the best solution.

Healing methods are great. They are all wonderful, but **dowsing is the only tool that will tell you which method will work in a given situation.**

Dowsing doesn't do the healing. It doesn't transform the energies. But you can see that in a way, it is more powerful than a healing method, because it tells you what method will work for your needs.

How many times have you done something 'good,' but it didn't work for you? How often have you invested in a supplement or treatment that did not heal you? Dowsing is the only method that will stop those kinds of mistakes. It will save you money, time and effort, and it will guide you to a faster healing process.

If you have not understood dowsing or health dowsing as we do, don't worry. Our approach to health dowsing is a practical, down-to-earth way to tap into your intuition to get information that will help you reach your health goals.

We will mention a variety of healing and transformational techniques, although this book is not a training in the use of intention or healing. Health dowsing has saved us time, effort, money and on a number of occasions, our health, and we believe that if you learn the techniques in this book, you can also experience great results with health dowsing.

Health Dowsing As A Specialty

HISTORICALLY, dowsing was mainly used to find water and minerals. In the 20th century, someone recognized that dowsing was simply seeking an answer to a question, so why not ask other questions when dowsing? This clever observation led to an explosion of dowsing applications: asking about health, finding lost objects, dowsing about energies, and relationship and financial dowsing, among others.

Organizations like the American Society of Dowsers (ASD) found themselves swamped with interest, most of it not about water dowsing. Faced with rapid growth in a subject the original members were not schooled in, they worked to train dowsers based on water dowsing principles. But unlike water dowsing, other types of dowsing were complex. Water dowsers basically ask one question over and over: Where's the water? Same for mineral dowsers. Dowsers seeking buried pipes and cables were able to adapt water dowsing principles to their needs, but what about those who wanted to find out all about their health or how to fix their finances?

Since training usually consisted of learning to get a yes/no response with a tool, people graduated from class unprepared to dive into the more complex applications of dowsing. They didn't know how to formulate good dowsing questions, nor how to become detached from wanting a certain answer. Health dowsing is perhaps the most complex and daunting dowsing application, so it requires the dowser to be not only competent, but masterful.

Each dowsing specialty has its own vocabulary, pitfalls and protocols. It can take years to become a truly masterful dowser in any given specialty, and that is assuming the dowser is studying and practicing often. A masterful water dowser has an accuracy of 90%+. But because each specialty is unique, a water dowser is not necessarily accurate in other types of dowsing. Many people operate under the misconception that if you can dowse at all, you can dowse accurately about anything. This is simply not true. Thus, there is a need for this book—for books and courses on any and every dowsing specialty—and the need for the teacher or writer to be masterful in that specialty.

There is no regulation or certification in dowsing, and we don't believe that would be useful in any case, but the dowsing student needs to do his/her due diligence before joining a course or reading a book so that time and money are not wasted. There are misinformed or greedy people who promote themselves as "Master Dowsers" and claim they will show you how to dowse successfully about money or relationships, when in reality, they are not experts in those fields. Do research on the authors of books and teachers of courses to convince yourself that they are masterful at what they are teaching or talking about. Many of them seem to think if they can get consistent dowsing answers about one topic, that makes them Master Dowsers who can dowse well about anything. In our experience, this is just not true.

We've been health dowsing for ourselves, our pets and our clients for nearly twenty years before we wrote this book, and we expect to continue to learn, grow and improve our accuracy in the future through practice, study and evaluation of our results, as will you. We don't claim to be experts at finding lost objects, siting wells or dowsing about money, because we don't have enough experience in those topics, so you won't see us writing books about them.

So if health dowsing is your passion, great, but don't assume that means you will be adept in all other dowsing specialties. You will probably be drawn to one or two dowsing applications, and if you invest time in learning them, you can master them, and that will give you great satisfaction. But don't make the mistake of thinking that will make you masterful in all dowsing applications.

∿

Basic Dowsing Training

THIS GUIDE IS NOT A DOWSING COURSE. LEARNING to dowse is very straightforward, but you will get better results if you get good training. This section is just a refresher of the basics you should have already mastered.

Dowsing involves several steps:

1. Be clear about your goal
2. Form a good question that is very detailed and specific and has a yes or no answer
3. Focus on the question and empty your mind (this is called

getting into a dowsing state)
4. Be curious but not attached to what the answer is
5. Receive the answer
6. If possible, confirm the answer

Steps 1-4 seem pretty easy to understand, though each one involves work and practice to master. Make a mistake at any step, and your answer will probably be incorrect.

Step 5, the actual answer, is just a small part of the process, but it may be the part which seems the most strange to you. When you dowse, you can either use a tool like a pendulum, or you can dowse without a tool, using some part of your body to give you the answer (the latter is what kinesiologists do). Step 5 is when you switch from rational mode to intuitional mode, and that shift is vital for success.

We prefer to teach and use deviceless dowsing methods, that is, methods that do not use a tool like a pendulum. Dowsing without a tool is closest to the skill in its natural form and has been shown to involve a greater variety of brain waves than pendulum dowsing. There are many methods of deviceless dowsing, but one of the most common and most reliable is the Body Sway. The Body Sway uses the forward or backward motion of your body to indicate 'yes' or 'no.'

Give it a try. Stand straight, relaxed, feet shoulder width apart. Close your eyes. Breathe normally. Think of the city or country you were born in. Ask, "Was I born in _____?" (Fill in the blank with the correct answer.) Wait in a curious and detached way to see what your body does. Forward is usually 'yes.' Did you get forward motion?

Don't be upset if you did not. Maybe your 'yes' is backward motion. Check out your 'no' answer by asking the question again, but this time, insert an answer you know is wrong for your birthplace. As long as you get a different motion for 'yes' and 'no,' you can dowse and get an answer.

How accurate your answer will be depends on how good and clear your question is, how detached and focused you are and a number of other factors we won't go into here, but are covered in any comprehensive dowsing course.

The purpose of this demonstration was to show you that it is possible to tap into your intuition in a focused way and get an answer to a question right now. We used your birthplace, because it's easy and you know what is right and wrong. When you dowse about health issues, you won't know if your answer is right or wrong, which is why we urge you to get further training.

Scales are used in dowsing to go beyond yes/no answers and find out the level of intensity of a noxious energy or a given course of action. There are many kinds of scales, but 0-10 and +10 to -10 are most common. Finding out a number value consists of asking what the intensity is and either saying each number until you get 'yes,' pendulum dowsing a chart that shows the numbers, or just thinking the numbers in your head and going through them as a list until you get a 'yes.' Scales are vital in health dowsing, as they provide detailed information. We go into more detail on these topics in the 'Dowsing Techniques' chapter.

Last, but not least, Step 6, confirming your dowsing answer, builds confidence and helps you improve your technique. Confirmation usually comes later on when dowsing for health. You will either see good results or you will feel your dowsing was wrong based on outcomes. If the former, your confidence in dowsing will grow. If the latter, you have the opportunity to go back, look at what you did and improve your technique. Keeping a dowsing journal will help you to benefit from both successes and 'failures'.

Never assume your answers are always right, but don't be afraid to make mistakes. You can learn a lot from them. Try to avoid dowsing too far above your level of confidence, and always get a second or third opinion on important questions. This will mitigate the bad effects of dowsing mistakes and help you gain confidence and mastery.

History Of Dowsing For Health

IN THE SECOND half of the 20th century, dowsing as a tool expanded beyond water witching and other physical searches (as for minerals and diamonds) when people realized that dowsing is simply that—a search. Dowsing for water, diamonds and minerals persisted over the centuries for one reason: it works. Because it works, dowsing increased profits of diamond and mineral companies, and it increased success of well-diggers, whose fees are not inconsiderable.

Long before the advent of the scientific method, which doesn't adapt to all situations, people used empirical observations to decide what worked and what didn't, and using dowsing to find minerals and water persisted because the results are immediately obvious to even the most skeptical individual. Maybe historically, dowsing was used for many other subjects, but no written record has been left. Many of the applications we now have for dowsing don't always give obvious physical proof of dowsing's efficacy, and that means a certain amount of faith is required, and most people want constant physical proof or at least to have Science say it works.

Dowsing has stood the test of time, but it doesn't adapt well to scientific validation, because it is a human activity rather than a natural phenomenon that exists outside of humans. Also, trying to dowse in artificial conditions is not equal to dowsing in real life situations, so laboratory experiments tend to fail, and in any case, are not real dowsing, simply because they are artificial situations.

The scientific method is historically in its infancy, so don't be persuaded to think that only by scientific validation can something be worthwhile or real. At some future time, perhaps Science will advance enough that it can meaningfully study things like dowsing, but for now, we accept the long history of acceptance of dowsing for certain applications as enough proof to make it worth investigating and learning. Once you have learned to dowse accurately and can see how it expands your ability to make good choices, you won't care whether Science has 'proven' it or not. You will get positive proof often enough to keep you dowsing, and that's all that will matter to you.

Very little has been written about dowsing historically, and it isn't recorded who first saw the pattern of dowsing being a search for answers, but that person's insight made possible all the dowsing applications we have today, because each dowsing specialty is simply a search for answers to questions the rational mind cannot answer. Finding lost objects, discovering a remedy for a health problem, picking a good stock to buy and choosing a career are all based on gathering enough information to succeed, and dowsing provides answers that cannot be gotten in other ways.

Health dowsing has evolved into the most popular dowsing application, as health is almost every dowser's #1 priority. The reason health dowsing is not practiced a lot and rarely practiced masterfully is that it is many times harder to master health dowsing than to master water dowsing.

Dowsing for water, diamonds and minerals involves skill, but the skill set is small compared to what you need for health dowsing. Usually, for these types of dowsing, you are dowsing for the same thing every time you dowse. Water dowsers always dowse for underground water. You use the same question or questions and the same basic techniques. There isn't a huge body of knowledge you need to master in order to find underground water, in part because you don't have to think up good questions for each new case. You use the same question every time you search for water, or you use one that is only slightly different.

The difference in skill sets between water dowsing and health dowsing is like the difference between being able to shoot baskets and playing a good game of basketball. This is not to demean water dowsing, but it's important to realize each dowsing application has its own terminology, techniques and pitfalls. And some dowsing applications are easier to master than others. Health dowsing is one of the most challenging, because it requires a good knowledge of human biology as well as the ability to craft questions for an infinite variety of situations. Furthermore, it demands a level of detachment that can be quite challenging if you are dowsing life and death issues, which isn't likely to come up when water dowsing or dowsing lost objects.

Because health dowsing is so challenging a field, it discourages people from seeking mastery, because we live in a culture of instant gratification. Health dowsing can take years to master, and even masters continue to learn and grow.

Although there have been decades of people dowsing for health, there are very few books or courses available to students, so it hasn't really matured. I took one basic health dowsing course in the 90s, and I can't recall finding a single good book on health dowsing during that time, and believe me, I looked. At that time and in the early years of the 21st century, much of my learning took the form of trial and error, which is slow and painful. One must relentlessly pursue mastery, practicing, making mistakes, learning from them, discussing techniques and results with other dowsers in order to improve accuracy. At the time of this writing (2018), there are still only a few good books and even fewer courses on health dowsing. This book aims to condense as much of our expertise as possible so that you may have a much shorter, smoother path to mastery than we did.

At this point in time, health dowsing has not evolved enough that there is even discussion, much less agreement, about how to best teach or even practice health dowsing. We are in the infancy of a priceless discipline, and hopefully, more people will master it and share its benefits widely in the coming years.

While dowsing is not a healing method, it is a great tool for healers. The longest history of the use of dowsing in healing is that of chiropractors using kinesiology. Kinesiology, also called muscle testing, was developed in 1964 by Dr. George Goodheart. He stumbled on the fact that the body tries to tell us in various ways, particularly with weak muscles, that something is out of balance and needs healing.

Kinesiology, like dowsing, gets answers via subtle body movements. In muscle testing, weak means 'bad' or 'no' and strong means 'good' or 'yes'. With deviceless dowsing (which is what kinesiology is), depending on the method, you rely on different body movements for 'yes' and 'no' replies. If you use a tool when dowsing, the tool is merely an amplifier of the subtle body movements that indicate 'yes' or 'no'.

Muscle testing usually requires two people: the doctor and the patient. Dowsing can be used by a single person for herself, or for a client in person or at a distance. Kinesiology can be considered a special application of dowsing that uses another person's body to get a yes/no answer via a strong or weak muscle response. Kinesiology (like dowsing) is not always used for health, but it is most widely practiced by health care professionals.

Healing methods like Touch For Health and The Emotion Code incorporate dowsing or muscle testing into their technique, not to heal, but to get answers that lead to successful treatment. Note that chiropractors never claim muscle testing (dowsing) is a healing method. They apply a fix of some kind to whatever problem dowsing reveals to them.

Health Dowsing is a new and challenging skill to learn, and there are not a lot of reliable resources for learning it at this time. We hope that will change in the future.

Tool Use

WE ARE advocates of deviceless dowsing, that is, dowsing without a tool, but in certain situations, the use of a tool will enhance your dowsing success. While a lot of your health dowsing can be done without a tool, there are some situations where a pendulum will come in quite handy.

WHEN TO CHOOSE Deviceless Dowsing

Practice your deviceless dowsing frequently, until you become confident with it. Use it as much as possible in all types of dowsing. There are many deviceless techniques, so find one or two that work well for you, and hone your skill with those methods.

Deviceless techniques work great for health dowsing questions that use a scale or yes/no answer, but are not ideal for chart dowsing.

WHEN TO USE A Pendulum

If you are very new to health dowsing and lack confidence or training in health, you might find it useful to use charts when searching for specific answers, like the best therapy or supplement. A pendulum is needed for chart dowsing, because you need a way to indicate which item on the chart is the answer.

An alternative is to use lists instead of charts. You can use a deviceless technique to dowse a list much easier than when dowsing a chart. Charts and lists basically are just different ways of displaying a lot of choices.

Another time a pendulum comes in handy is when you are dowsing chakras, something we discuss in the 'Dowsing Protocols' chapter.

If you are using a sketch of the human body or an animal's body to find the root cause of a problem, a pendulum can be used, though you can also use deviceless techniques.

Of course, if you are not confident about deviceless dowsing, you can always use a pendulum for all your health dowsing.

Dowsing Proficiency

BEING proficient in dowsing is a prerequisite for a health dowser. This statement may frighten you, because perhaps you are not yet a confident dowser. All new dowsers (at least the smart ones) go through a period of doubt and low self-confidence. This is a reflection of their awareness that they are new, haven't mastered technique yet, and to some extent, are still questioning how dowsing can even work.

Those who persevere become more confident and master proper technique and see for themselves how amazing dowsing is as a tool for health. Anyone can become proficient as a dowser, but it takes time and practice and study. Don't be discouraged if you are still in the beginning of your dowsing journey. If you persist, you will gain confidence, and your accuracy will improve.

Health dowsing should not be undertaken by newbies except in rare situations. If you feel you are a 'natural' at dowsing, because you are really accurate, and you have significant training in biology or health, then you can undertake the simpler health dowsing techniques early on. Do not, however, attempt to dowse about anything serious until you are sure your accuracy and technique are adequate to the task, because advanced health dowsing requires a high level of proficiency. Better safe than sorry.

2

USING DOWSING EFFECTIVELY FOR YOUR HEALTH

Prerequisites

Do you have all the prerequisites to dive into health dowsing? Below is a list that will guide you. Be honest about your experience and proficiency and fill in any blanks by reading, studying and practicing.

If you are competent at all of the following, you are ready to begin dowsing for health:

- You are an accurate dowser, meaning in certain specialties, 90% or higher
- You have learned how to be detached when dowsing, so that whatever the answer, you can allow it to come through
- You are good at using scales when dowsing
- You are competent at list or chart dowsing
- You understand how to form a good dowsing question
- You are willing to learn from your mistakes, rather than fear making mistakes
- You have an open mind about what creates good health

- You have a good foundation in the basics of health and human biology

Level Of Education

One of the most common questions we are asked is do you need a degree in Biology or do you need to be a doctor to be an accurate health dowser? This is a good question. And the answer will vary depending on the dowser.

Maggie has two degrees in Biology and has read avidly about all aspects of human health and healing. For her, having an education in health and biology have been an asset as a health dowser. This is in part because she was trained as a scientist and also taught to think rationally. By falling back on her education, she can health dowse within the framework of her educational background, which plays to her personality and preferences.

Medical intuitives often are people who have not had an education in Biology, yet they are amazingly accurate. This may relate in part to their preference for using the intuitive faculty over the rational.

Regardless of whether you are highly educated in health or not, you can still be a very accurate health dowser. Nigel doesn't have degrees in Biology, yet he is accomplished at dowsing for health, and in fact was professionally dowsing for health in the UK before he met Maggie.

It's important to note that as with any skill, some people take to health dowsing rapidly with very little training and get good results. The percentage of folks who can do this is very small, but you may be one of the lucky ones who is a dowsing prodigy.

It may be a bit unsatisfying for you to hear that we aren't going to say you have to know this or that or take this or that course in order to be a competent health dowser, but the truth is that it depends on you. You are an individual, and you need to do what works for you.

If you are the type who needs to have training in order to feel safe or competent doing something, then get training. If you are less concerned about having a diploma or being able to say you've read thousands of books on the topic, then a simple understanding of human health may be adequate for you.

At a minimum, we recommend that you familiarize yourself with basic human biology and health topics. It will be more enjoyable for you if you understand the basics about organs and systems and their function, but you might find that ongoing study, reading and online trainings are enough to help you.

If you only want to focus on resolving health issues, and you have no interest in causes, it is possible to do health dowsing well as long as your technique is good and you avoid anything to do with 'diagnosis' of cause. A health dowser can determine the best remedy for a situation without knowing what the cause is, but most dowsers will feel more comfortable if they can explain and understand why they got the answer they did.

Using Dowsing For Yourself

YOUR HEALTH IS important to you, and you don't want to ignore a symptom that is begging for outside help, but you also don't want to waste time, sick leave and money on something that will resolve itself without outside intervention. Dowsing comes to your rescue in those situations.

Dowsing is not 100% accurate. Nothing is. But dowsing is way more accurate than an educated guess, because it draws on your intuitive sensing abilities, which have been honed sharply by dowsing often. Dowsing connects you to a source of information that will guide you to the best action to take for your goals, as long as you can dowse well.

We recommend that you use dowsing at those times when it isn't obvious what to do. We suggest you master the techniques in this book so that you have them at your fingertips when you need them. Doing regular 'checkups' using dowsing will help you gain confidence and also give you a feel for your body and your health, so that when you need to fall back on your dowsing skills, you will be ready.

～

Combining With Healing Methods

DOWSING IS NOT A HEALING METHOD. If this contradicts what you have been told, don't get upset. There is a lot of confusion among dowsers due to the lack of consistency in definitions and teaching methods. At least one prominent dowsing guru in the past used intention and dowsing together in courses, and if not meaning to equate the two, the inference most students made rapidly caused them to think dowsing was the same thing as using intention to make changes.

In the late 90's, in the health dowsing course I took, the teacher made it clear when he dowsed for details of health problems and when he shifted gears and used intention or another method like SRT (Spiritual Response Therapy) to transform energy. Often, he used his pendulum to indicate when the transformation was complete, but he never stated nor implied that the pendulum was doing any of the work, or that the transformation of energy was part of the dowsing process. He could just as simply have used deviceless dowsing, but wanted us to see the 'yes' of the pendulum so that we could see how long it took to transform the energy. When you think about such a demonstration, you can see how a student could mistakenly think that dowsing was the whole process if the teacher wasn't careful to explain steps, especially if he used a pendulum or tool.

If you wish to learn how to power intention, that is a great skill to have, and we encourage you to do so, but intention is a healing or energy transformation method. It is not part of dowsing. Dowsing is a way of getting answers that will help you determine a proper course of action for your health. Dowsing combines well with any healing method, including intention (if you know how to power it).

It helps if you have several healing methods at hand, because there is no one method that heals everything. You can use dowsing to determine which healing method will give you the best results with the fewest side effects.

It doesn't matter whether you use conventional medicine, holistic medicine or real woo-woo methods, dowsing is the way to guide you through the many choices you face when you have a medical issue and aren't sure what to do to resolve it. While dowsing is regarded as a New Age technique, it is a valuable tool when working within any medical paradigm. The only caveat is that if you intend to rely on dowsing, you will want to choose a medical professional who will accept your participation and also respect your input.

In summary, here is how dowsing fits into your healing journey:

- You can dowse to determine if your symptom is a sign of dis-ease
- Use dowsing to figure out the cause of your symptom, if so
- Dowsing can help you determine the efficacy of consulting a doctor
- If the process is benign, use dowsing to find out how you can support the process and make it smoother
- Dowsing will help you choose a healing technique or a therapy or remedy for your problem if you determine you can solve it yourself
- You can find out the level of side effects and effectiveness of any therapy or medicine with dowsing

- It is possible to determine how long the healing process will take by dowsing
- You can use dowsing to fine tune your actions during the healing process

Do You Need A Doctor?

The most important thing dowsing can help you decide is whether you need to go to a doctor or vet for a particular health issue. Being able to dowse just this one question accurately can save you tons of money, lots of time and worry, and maybe even save your life or that of a loved one.

The caveat is that you must be an accurate dowser. This theme repeats throughout the book, and we urge you to take every opportunity to dowse about your health on minor and simple issues so that when the time comes, you have confidence and accuracy for the harder questions.

You are an individual. Not everyone will go to a doctor for the same symptoms. You know your own body and that of your children and pets better than a doctor who sees them maybe once or twice a year. You have learned the patterns of dis-ease and healing in your own body, and if you have children or pets, you have also gained a lot of knowledge about their bodies as well.

How well-off you are financially and what type of insurance, if any, you have will play a part in your decision about going to a doctor or vet. Whether you have time or the ability to take time off will also play a role in your choice. But most of all, your knowledge of the medical history of the person will contribute to whether you feel a need to consult a professional.

Even if you are fully aware of all these factors, you still won't always be able to guess whether it's a good investment or not, and that's where dowsing comes in. Your needs and your situation are unique, and dowsing will help you make the right choice for your goals.

3
WHAT IS HEALTH?

Our Approach To Health

You will get the most out of this book and its contents if you see health as we do, but even if you are very conventional in your outlook, you can still use many of the protocols to help you make better health choices so that you can improve your health.

Our approach to health is constantly evolving in response to our experiences and what we have learned from them, so in describing our approach here, we are not saying it is the one true way to achieve your health goals. There are many paths to good health, and what is most important is that you have clear intentions and commit to doing whatever it takes to achieve your goals. No matter what path you take on your healing journey, you can create a successful outcome, and you will learn a lot along the way.

In this section, we want to share some of the beliefs and perspectives that have helped us get the most out of health dowsing. Some will resonate with you; some may not. Remember we are all works in progress, and there are many ways to achieve good health. We present these ideas as potentially useful. You will know which ones to follow if you listen to your heart.

Good health and well-being are natural states, not impossible goals. Do not think of yourself as broken or defective, no matter what your health challenge. Negative thinking cements the problem in place. Whatever you are currently experiencing is just that, an experience. Do not identify with it. You are able to express good health. That is the belief you want to focus on.

Sometimes something that feels bad is good for you. Not every symptom is a sign of illness or dis-ease. Some positive processes create discomfort and even pain. Never assume you are sick or unwell just because you don't feel quite right. Use dowsing (see the 'Is It Good Or Bad?' section in the 'Dowsing Protocols' chapter) to find out, because that will help you choose a more effective path to resolving it.

You are more powerful than you think. It doesn't matter how educated or smart you are or are not. You know your body better than anyone else, and that gives you power that no one else has. You can learn the language of your body and allow it to guide you to good health. Do not give your power away.

Being responsible for your health means you are able to adapt, not that you are to blame for your experiences. You are not a victim. You are not to blame. You have the ability to respond to whatever health challenge you face and overcome it. Victims can't do that. Only by accepting your power will you find the ability to improve your health or create the health you want.

Good health begins in the subtle energy body and is affected by many invisible energies within and without. To us, this is a foundational belief. If all you treat are physical symptoms, the energies generally don't change, or they morph into another set of symptoms. You must rebalance and heal the energies in order to 'cure' a condition permanently. There are invisible factors affecting your health that are external to you, such as EMFs, and there are internal ones, like beliefs and programming. We find it useful to work not only on the proximate cause of a health problem, but the root cause, as well.

Your body has an amazing capacity for self-healing. Don't get caught up in trying to find and fix every little thing that you think is blocking you from experiencing good health. Focusing on what you don't want and what is wrong will not easily lead you to good health. Spend more time focusing on your goals than on what's wrong. What do you want to experience? Use dowsing to help you find out how to do that.

The natural way to better health is usually the gentlest, least risky and most effective way, but it requires patience. The human body has evolved to respond well to natural remedies, but modern life has thrown off the subtle sensitivities by introducing toxins, chemicals, EMFs and habits that create imbalance, stress and bad health. Living as naturally as possible is your best approach for achieving optimal health. This is simple, but not always easy to do.

Prevention is the best way to enjoy good health. Being conscious is a requirement. Self-awareness is needed. If it were easy, everyone would be doing it. Most people are too un-conscious or lazy to put effort into health up front, but it is the best way to enjoy good health consistently. Don't kick yourself if you find it hard to stay the course. Do your best, and keep making an effort to become more conscious and self-aware as you journey to excellent health.

We all need outside help from time to time. No matter how good a health dowser you are or how healthy you are, there will be times when you need outside help. Don't regard that as a failing. Learn to use dowsing and intuition to know when to ask for help.

Time and space are human constructs that can be overridden. You don't have to create your future from past experiences. Dowsing is like time-traveling or action at a distance. And when you choose a healing method, you can send healing intentions to the past or to another continent if that method is an energy transformation method.

The most important factor for your health is what you think and believe. When it comes down to it, you can have the best diet and exercise regimen, you can live in the cleanest environment and still be terribly ill. The flip side is you can live among toxins and negative health influences and still be healthy. Monitor your beliefs, because they will be your greatest allies or your most formidable enemies.

We believe in the Law Of Attraction and try to apply it in our daily life. It takes a lot of time to understand and apply the Law Of Attraction, but we have found it works. We highly recommend it as a way of seeing the world and how it works and how you can create the outcomes you desire. It is a journey, just like healing, so be patient. The basic premise is like attracts like energy. This is why we urge you to focus on what you intend to create, not what is 'wrong' or bothersome. What you focus on expands.

Good health can be simple and easy to experience. We start out on our healing journey wishing it would be easy and maybe even grasping at scams and claims that promise quick results. Then when they don't deliver, we knuckle down and commit to doing whatever it takes, which usually includes hard work, a lot of time and effort and a considerable amount of money. In other words, a lot of personal investment. Then, after a time, if we keep growing, we arrive back at where we began, as we realize we are making it hard due to our programming and beliefs and fears, and as we set those aside and truly believe good health is simple to achieve, things begin to get easier, because we truly believe it can be simple instead of just wishing it were so.

Having said all this, in the sections that follow, we guide you to think deeply about what health is to you and then create your own health goals. Remember, there are many paths to health. You must choose what resonates with you, but be open to change, because we have found that improving health and healing dis-ease requires a change of mind more than anything else.

∼

What Is Health To You?

ONE OF THE most important questions you can answer is what does health mean to you? Your definition of health will drive your goals and your choices. So the first thing you need to do is decide what is health to you, because if you don't know that, dowsing can lead you to disappointing or frustrating results.

On the face of it, 'what is health to you?' may seem a silly question. But it isn't. Do you define health as the absence of pain? The absence of disease? Or do you define health as having something tangible, like plenty of energy to do what you feel like, feeling comfortable in your body, being flexible and youthful?

In the US, the conventional medical system is based on a definition of health that relates to not having pain or symptoms. For that reason, much of what conventional health care offers is aimed at erasing symptoms and pain. Conventional medicine is poor at dealing with degenerative diseases and conditions caused by lifestyle, because it does not address the cause of a health problem. Instead, it aims to eradicate the symptom.

If you have a migraine, conventional medicine gives you a pill to eliminate the pain. If you have heavy periods, you get pain killers to minimize the cramps. If you get indigestion, they prescribe an antacid or acid blocker so your stomach won't hurt.

In our opinion, this approach is a weakness in conventional medicine. Conventional medicine is excellent at dealing with trauma and severe infections, but the causes of those things tend to be relatively simple, acute and sudden in onset, not related to lifestyle.

The bone is broken, so splint it. There are bacteria rampaging in your body, so kill them.

If your definition of health is just not having pain, then your energy will resonate with a more conventional outlook. This is especially true if you don't want to change anything in your life in order to be healthy.

Dowsing can still be very helpful to you if you have a conventional approach to health. You probably won't use it to sleuth out the cause of a health issue, but you will find it useful for selecting the right therapy or pill and for measuring side effects of drugs or surgery.

What if your definition of health is more proactive and less about the absence of something you don't want? Your concept of health may grow and deepen over time. At first you may just want the energy to be able to do your work and keep up with your kids. But once you achieve that, you will see that you can modify your definition and say you'd like to have the energy for a hobby and for going out dancing on a Saturday night, that you'd like to feel young and flexible and be able to lift a 40 lb. bag of dog food without help.

Allow yourself to start at whatever points feels best to you, but be aware that you can change or add to that definition at any time, and the more specific you are, the more likely you are to get good results. If you are proactive about creating excellent health and you are specific about your goals, dowsing is a priceless tool for helping you to reach them.

EXERCISE

Sit down and think about what health means to you. Don't just think of the symptoms you wish would disappear. How would you like to feel instead? What would you like to be able to do? Think big. Write it down. Come back later and add to it as needed. Tune in and see if your definition is truly in alignment with what you want to experience and your level of commitment. Your definition of health is the target you are aiming at, so be specific. Note that the harder it is for you to put into words what you want to experience, what good health means to you in positive terms, the more likely it is that you have been focusing on what you don't want. This exercise will refocus your attention on the positive, and that is a big first step towards positive outcomes.

∽

Setting Health Goals

Many of us feel it's tedious or boring to set goals. Maybe it's also daunting, because then we know we have to measure our results, and we may 'fail'. No one likes to fail, but you can't succeed unless you are also able to fail. When things don't work out as planned, it helps us to create a new program or strategy for reaching our goals. This is a natural part of the healing process or any journey.

Now that you've defined what health means to you, you are ready to set health goals. Your goals should be measurable and reasonable (which means you believe they are attainable). It is also important to be willing to let your goals evolve over time.

When setting goals, we suggest that you not use something negative as your way to measure your progress. Losing weight is a good example. Focusing on losing weight is a negative outlook, as it stems from a judgment about excess weight. It tends to focus you on the 'reality' that you aren't yet slim and trim every time you step on a scale. This causes you to vibrate with lack and that makes your goal harder to attain.

What is a more positive goal? What would you do if you were in good physical condition or slim and trim that you cannot do now? Something you really desire. You might wish you could climb a set of stairs easily, since right now, you get out of breath. That is measurable. Perhaps you wish you could easily lift a 40 lb. sack of dog food. If your goal is to get in shape, think about what you intend to do once you are in shape, and make that your goal. If it is hard to get specific about your positive goal, this is a sign that you have been dwelling on what you don't want instead of what you do want. Shift that focus.

Set a reasonable time frame for your goals to be attained. Don't set yourself up for failure.

Plan a program that you think will help you attain those goals. This is where dowsing is priceless. Then stick to that program and measure results.

Getting on a scale every day is not likely to make you feel like a success. It takes time to lose weight. Wouldn't it be better if you let the pounds slip away and focus instead on becoming stronger and more capable?

Staying with the goal of being in shape, since that is something many people struggle with, what if your goal is to feel better about how you look each time you see yourself in the mirror? That is measurable, too. But unlike a physical fitness program, that goal will require some personal energy shifting.

Here's an example: a client once told us she wanted to lose weight. I asked her a lot of questions, including when the excess weight had been put on. She replied that she remembered quite clearly. She had been slim and trim until she was in her teens, and her brother made an offhand remark one day that she was so attractive, she'd soon have to beat men off with a stick. This statement traumatized her at some level, though she hadn't been consciously aware of that until we discussed it. She said she almost immediately began to put on weight after her brother said that. She figured it was a subconscious effort to put men off, a sort of suit of armor for protection from unwanted advances. No diet or exercise program had ever given her success, because her main problem was emotional. By addressing her fear of unwanted advances, she was able to feel safe being more slim and trim.

There are many emotional components to excess weight. You will need to select a method that will help you transform emotions that are blocking weight loss, because that is the only way you will ever reach your goal. It isn't the extra weight that makes you hate how you look; it's the low self-esteem or lack of self-worth or fear in general that is expressing through that symptom. Dowsing will help you choose the right method for your needs.

This example illustrates that changing your health in any way is likely to include both physical and emotional aspects, and dowsing will help you plan a good program. Another factor to consider is your energetic environment, which can be evaluated via dowsing. You are probably beginning to get the picture that health dowsing is way more valuable than any healing method. It is a tool you will use every step of the way on your journey.

EXERCISE

Take some time to think about your health goals. You should have already written in your journal what health means to you, but that is in general terms and could take years to experience. Think about your concept of health, and write down goals for next month and next year. Depending on your challenge, you might do weekly goals, or you may have goals for farther out than one year. Write them down in detail and make sure they seem reasonable to you and that they are measurable.

Use your journal to chart your progress. Be sure to include your mental and emotional state. You might want to note things you have done as part of your program, like doing Reiki or tapping. Note any physical measures that show progress.

What if your goals have to do with something you can't easily measure? If your goal is something nebulous, like wanting to feel significantly more energetic, use a 0 to 10 scale to assign a number that matches how you feel each day. You could measure in the morning or at night before bed. You could use one number to average how you felt all day, or you could use a number to represent the most energetic you felt that day. Write down how you want to define the scale in as much detail as possible. Then assign a number each day, without cheating. If the numbers improve, that is a sign you are doing better. This subjective method is good about things that cannot be measured physically, and it is a valid way of charting progress if you define the scale clearly at the outset.

Physical Or Energetic?

WE BELIEVE, as many people do, that all physical symptoms begin in the subtle energy body, so that if you want to be healthy, you need to address not only the physical body, but energy, as well. If all you do is treat the physical body, in essence, you are not treating the root cause of your health problem. The physical body needs your support during the healing process, but solely doing physical remedies is usually not a permanent fix for a health problem.

This is true even if your health problem is something like an accident that led to a broken bone. An accident holds a certain pattern of energy that is detrimental, and where you are injured is an energetic message about an energy imbalance in your system. Even the most acute and seemingly random health issue is a message about your energy system.

After an energetic imbalance or issue has been around for a while, it begins to manifest in the physical body. At that point, it is wise to treat both the energetic cause and the physical body itself for faster healing. You could just treat the root cause, but we have found that the body appreciates a little help in the healing process. So we suggest you do both.

Dowsing will help you figure out how to approach both aspects of health for best results. In the Resources section, we mention books that we have found helpful for decoding physical health symptoms to find the energetic issue.

∼

Prevention vs. Fixing

WE MENTIONED EARLIER that depending on your health paradigm, you may be focused on fixing problems or preventing them (though of course, you can do both). Either way, dowsing will come in very handy.

We personally believe in preventing imbalances that lead to dis-ease. We look at it like this: you are going to invest time, effort and probably money in fixing a health problem once it arrives, so why not invest beforehand and make sure it doesn't happen? That way, you can have optimal health.

You need to choose which approach you are going to take, as that will determine which medical paradigm you follow. If you are into prevention, you won't get along as well with the conventional medical system, which is focused on eradicating symptoms. You will find yourself at odds with what your doctor wants you to do, and it isn't that he's a bad person; it's that you and he aren't starting with the same values and assumptions.

If you are into prevention, a holistic professional may be your best bet. Some will say that insurance doesn't cover that sort of care, but what does it matter? You need to align with a system that resonates with your beliefs, or you will constantly be in conflict and stressed out. Fortunately, there is a lot you can do on your own without a professional, as prevention is about lifestyle choices, and we all make choices every day.

Fixing problems, on the other hand, can be costly if you choose a natural approach. (Thinking about prevention vs. fixing problems after they show up is an example of the choice you have about living consciously or just sailing through life without thinking much, and then doing whatever 'experts' say when things go wrong. The unconscious life is the one most people live, but it isn't really because they thought about it and said, "Hey, living unconsciously is best." If you really start to think deeply about the question of living consciously and creating what you think of as good health, you will find it hard to go back to being unconscious.)

We are not saying that conventional medicine is always about being unconscious, nor is natural medicine always driven by conscious living. But when speaking generally, the paradigm of the conventional system appeals to the unconscious lifestyle, which is most common, while the natural health system appeals more to those who want to live consciously, and that is why it will probably never be the paradigm of the majority. We are living in an interesting time when these two paradigms are battling for people's dollars, and since governments are not motivated to have highly conscious citizens, the conventional approach gets the upper hand, so conscious people are faced with having to make a bigger financial investment in their health if they require professional help. This leads to confusion about what to do when illness strikes.

We have worked with clients who tried to blend their holistic living approach with conventional practitioners when they fell ill, and in most cases, it led to them being told to find another doctor or else they had to take a lot of verbal abuse if they were honest about their viewpoint or tried to participate in the healing process. At the very least, they were stressed out, because they didn't really like or believe in doing what the doctor said. If you can find an integrative doctor, that will usually blunt the negativity you will face, but even then, you will be asked to choose. Do you want to take a pill or fix the cause? Even some holistic doctors are now focusing more on giving you relief from symptoms, because there is such a great demand for that.

If you choose the prevention route 100%, you will discover that at some point you will create such good health that you hardly ever need a doctor. And that's a good thing. If your health is messed up, you will want to consult with professionals to get you back on track, but your long term goal will be not to need to go to a doctor often. And you will reach that goal.

If on the other hand, you prefer to use conventional medicine, and you just want to fix a symptom so it goes away, you can still use dowsing to find a good doctor, to test a therapy or drug and to measure side effects in advance. We don't believe this approach creates good health for most people, but it is your choice how you want to use health dowsing. Dowsing is a valuable method, no matter what your beliefs.

EXERCISE

What is your outlook on health? Are you more in alignment with a conventional or natural health approach? Write it down.

Do you think that having health insurance means you must use the current health system whenever you have a health issue? If so, why? If not, why not? Just make sure your answer isn't about money, as that is not a good reason to do anything.

Are you concerned about having the resources (time, money and intelligence) to take charge of your health? The Universe provides what you ask for. If you are concerned, you would be wise to clear some emotions or beliefs and step into your power. This is a big goal, but you will be paralyzed if you see yourself as a helpless victim.

If you desire to create a holistic health team, look at your overall health and your goals and think about what types of professionals you might want on your team. If you aren't sure, get online and look up the definitions of various holistic professions. While many people are aware of what chiropractors do, you might not be able to define what a homeopath or osteopath or naturopath or functional medicine doctor does. Educate yourself so that you can then dowse about how to create a good team for your needs. At this point, don't worry about money; just get to know what types of holistic care are available in your area.

Have you ever gone to the doctor (conventional or holistic) and not liked what he or she recommended as treatment? Have you ever gotten treatment, drugs or surgery that went wrong? How could dowsing have helped you avoid this situation?

Has your doctor ever treated you like an imbecile, refused to listen to your opinion or acted like you had no vote in the healing process? Has your doctor ever threatened to 'fire' you if you disagreed with his opinion or methods? What did you do? Would you get another doctor in these situations?

These exercises are to help you clarify in your own mind what your values are, and to give you a chance to think about how you can live those values rather than mindlessly doing what everyone else does. Regardless of your personal preferences, you need to think about these questions before you need professional help, to allow the process to be more efficient and successful.

∼

Conventional vs. Holistic

THE BEST TIME TO decide which health paradigm you want to follow is **before** you desperately need health care. Once you get a bad diagnosis, fear kicks in and most people just fall back and do what they are told. If you want to take charge of your health, decide now what your approach will be and start living it. So complete the exercise in the previous section and do some serious thinking about the general approach you want to take to health.

We have been asked in the past about mixing conventional and holistic methods, and in general, we haven't found that it works well **on a given health issue.** Our experience shows that you are better off not trying to keep one foot in each camp, as if to hedge your bets on resolving a problem. Go conventional if that suits you; go natural if that resonates more.

This does not mean that if you are into natural health that you won't see a conventional doctor if you break your arm in a fall. It means that you will seek conventional help only when you feel it conveys an advantage over natural health professionals. Trauma is one of the major areas conventional medicine excels.

But it is different if you go to a conventional doctor for everything just because you paid for health insurance, but you don't really resonate with drugs and surgery, or because you are afraid of spending money on holistic health care. We believe that it is important to choose to work with professionals who think like you do, and while it is possible that you will use both holistic and conventional medicine in your life, we urge you to choose for the right reasons.

Fear and money are not the right reasons to go to anyone, conventional or holistic. Consult with someone because you believe you will get good results and you can work with that person because you are in agreement about good health and how to create it. If you do this, your chances of positive outcomes are very good, no matter what you choose.

Money

It's impossible to address the challenge of you taking charge of your health without talking about money. Money is the currency used in modern society to buy goods and services, and unless you have money, it's hard to get the things you want, including things to do with health.

Almost everyone has issues with money, because it represents a sort of nourishment that most of us feel unworthy of or uncertain about, at least on some level. Most people have issues of self-worth, or they reject life on earth for various reasons, or they judge it to be bad, or else they judge those who are successful financially, saying they are greedy and evil. You can't be financially well off if you have too many of these energies, and most people do.

You can decide to cling to those beliefs and use a lack of money as your excuse for not changing. You can pretend that if you had money, you'd follow a different path, as if the lack of money is to blame for your choices (or lack thereof). This is an illusion that many people have, and it gives them some level of comfort, but clinging to that belief means their life can never change.

You can't wait around for money to drop out of the sky before you make a change in your life. You need to decide to make a change, and then take whatever action you can, knowing that the Universe will support you. This doesn't mean charging supplements or chiropractor visits to your credit card. It means taking whatever action you can to move towards your goals, expecting resources to come along as needed along the way, but acting within your budget. This is not an easy thing for most of us to do, but it is necessary if we want to change.

We've been financially challenged ourselves, and we know how restrictive it can be. However, there is always something you can do that doesn't cost money to show your intention to the Universe and proceed towards your goals. The main thing you need for creating health is a willingness to invest. If you don't have money (or even if you do), we believe that investing time, thought and effort is critical for success.

Here are a few free or inexpensive things you could choose to do for your health. They cost mostly time and effort, which you can find if you really are committed:

- Stop drinking tap water. Get a filter for your faucet or a filter pitcher. Even if it's not top-of-the-line, it is an improvement.
- Go on walks in Nature. Get up early if you have to. Walking is a great exercise.
- Cut back on alcohol, smoking and sugar consumption. Yes, this will even save you money.
- Buy some books or go to free webinars or get a library card and start studying about health in whatever way appeals to you.
- Quit eating fast food. Or at least get a salad instead of a double cheeseburger made of mystery meat with GMO french fries.
- Learn a method like meditation, toning, self-hypnosis or tapping. They are easy to learn and in some cases, you can learn for free by searching online. Then practice the method regularly.
- Master proper dowsing technique so you can be a good health dowser.

If you did all of the above regularly, your vibration would be vastly different from someone who doesn't think, has no goals and sits around making excuses for not taking action to improve her health. The Universe responds to your vibration, so change that, and the resources will start coming in. Try to avoid focusing on lack, as that only causes more lack. It is truly amazing what you can do with very little money if you put your mind to it.

4

MAJOR FACTORS THAT AFFECT HEALTH

Introduction

Being aware of factors that impact health is an important part of becoming a good health dowser. An example is that if all you think about when you are looking for causes of health problems are dietary issues like allergies, toxins and deficiencies, or microorganisms like parasites and infection, you are going to miss out on a lot, because they are only small pieces of the complex health puzzle.

If you want to understand everything that can impact health, the best and most accurate perspective may be obtained by stepping way back, looking at the big picture and approaching health from the viewpoint of evolutionary biology. While most of the specific theories within the concept of evolution are not proven and there is still much to learn on this topic, there is validity to the overall concept that natural factors mold our biology over time, and that over many thousands, even millions, of years, we have adapted to thrive in the natural terran environment; in fact, our biology is woven into the fabric of life on earth in a complex way that we are only beginning to understand through our scientific investigations.

With this in mind, you need to look hard at 'modern' conveniences and changes that have not passed the test of thousands or millions of years of time and ask if they are possibly conflicting with what your body's natural needs are. You probably already do this to some extent if you are aware of things like toxins and fake foods. But the problem of health challenges is bigger than most people are aware. All of the factors covered in this chapter influence your health either positively or negatively, and if you are aware of these effects, you can choose the positive and improve your health.

Since scientific endeavors cost money, only those experiments and investigations that might yield income for the backers are likely to be undertaken, leaving what was once called 'pure science' to languish, even though it holds the key to understanding our biology and how our health is affected by our environment. Worse yet, research that points to detrimental effects of big corporations' products is buried or smeared to avert loss of profits, as health is a multibillion dollar industry. Then there's the fact that science hasn't figured out how to measure metaphysical factors like beliefs, thoughts and emotions and their effect on health. Therefore, instead of relying solely on scientific data, you need to use your own ability to think critically in addition to dowsing, and a good rule of thumb when you want to create better health is to ask yourself how you can best approximate conditions under which humans evolved to live on earth and thrive in Nature, because when you are most in tune with Nature, you are most likely to be healthy.

We have listed the subjects in this chapter in approximate order of importance. Since health, good or ill, starts in the energy body, your beliefs, emotions and thoughts are a big factor. Next, we discuss genetics and epigenetics. Genetics is the blueprint you've inherited that gives you a range of expression for your physical body. How it expresses that blueprint depends on epigenetics, which includes factors in the environment that can turn genes off and on or pass down inherited patterns. The energies in your environment are in a sense an epigenetic factor, because they will directly affect your physical body.

We list diet and nutrition (a key environmental factor) after environmental effects, because they deserve their own section. The old way of thinking about health would have put diet and nutrition first. "You are what you eat" was an old maxim. The fuel you give your body is very important to your health, but we have seen over the years that no matter how well someone eats and supplements and exercises, they can still have terrible health challenges. That's because the other factors in this chapter can overpower even the best diet.

We strive to be on top of the latest scientific research on health, but as time passes, you will need to update what we are suggesting here, as the understanding of health will evolve and grow richer. As long as you remain open-minded and flexible in your thinking, you will be able to avoid getting locked into ways of thinking that are limiting and won't serve you. The more you understand what can impact your health, the better your dowsing will be when looking for solutions to health challenges, and that means thinking of the big picture and asking how humans were designed to naturally thrive and use the body's amazing self-healing abilities.

Beliefs, Emotions & Weird Stuff

IT IS BECOMING MORE ACCEPTED that your subconscious beliefs and past trauma contribute greatly to your experience of reality, yet most people don't clearly understand the connection. Health is something most of us consciously desire to have, but the conscious mind isn't running the show. Your subconscious mind is, and it is chock-a-block full of faulty beliefs and programs and the results of trauma in this and past lives that affect your health. It isn't enough to consciously think healthy thoughts; you need to make sure your subconscious is on board with your health goals, because it gets the final say.

It may seem ridiculous to assert this, but here's an example. Ill health can have a lot of secondary benefits, meaning it isn't fun, but it can lead to outcomes that you may consciously or subconsciously desire. We had a client many years ago who had very poor health. She consulted with us on how to become more healthy, but she consciously admitted that she believed that if she got well, her husband would leave her. As a result, she couldn't seem to get well. Her illness had a secondary benefit that she consciously wanted more than she wanted health, and all her attempts at healing failed.

Another situation where ill health has benefits is if you are part of a self-centered family, being sick might be your only way to get attention, if you are a child. Or if you are a busy adult, being sick might be the only 'down time' you allow yourself, and without knowing it, ill health becomes a sort of vacation from overwork.

If a person finds that only via illness can she get attention, she may develop the belief that sickness=love, and at the subconscious (or even conscious) level, she may believe she must be sick to get love. This means she will be sick often. (It is also a sign of very low self-worth). This is a belief I had all through my childhood, and it led to me being ill frequently. Furthermore, any effort to be well will fail in this kind of situation, as being well is not as important as being loved.

Your subconscious beliefs will affect your thoughts. Unless you monitor your thoughts, they can cause you to resonate with ill health. By training your thoughts to resonate with good health, you encourage good health. Don't go around saying, "My back is killing me." Nor should you think that a symptom defines you. "*My* arthritis is acting up." Try to think of symptoms as temporary and focus on your health goals, not 'what is' at this time.

Another way beliefs can drag you down is if you believe fast food is bad for your health, but you eat it every day because of convenience. Your belief that what you are doing is bad will lead to bad health. This is not to say that ignorant people can eat anything and stay healthy; it's just that focusing on a negative belief will create a negative outcome for sure. If you are forced by circumstances to occasionally eat fast food, try like heck to enjoy it and think positive thoughts while doing so. Overall, try to match your actions to your beliefs. Don't smoke if you think it causes cancer. Don't drink to excess if you feel that is bad for your health. Avoid foods you think are toxic.

When you take action that you believe will improve your health, you are aligned with positive outcomes. You might ask, why is it that even if you are eating well, you are still sicker than most people who eat fast food daily? This would seem to indicate you have beliefs that may go beyond food that are affecting your health. A belief that the world is a dangerous place or a desire not to be here in physical form can manifest as ill health, as can the belief that you cannot or don't deserve to be nourished and supported.

If you don't have beliefs like that (dowsing can tell you), then ill health means there are other factors that are affecting you. Check out the other topics in this chapter. One that most people are unaware of is the horrible effect of non-native EMFs on the cells in your body and your physiology.

Knowing your parents' and ancestors' medical histories is useful, because epigenetics is showing us that your parents' and grandparents' experiences of trauma can be passed on to you, even though you did not experience that trauma yourself. Trauma tends to create beliefs, many of them faulty, and also can lead to symptoms of ill health. Just like programming in school and at home affects your outlook, so do the past traumas of your ancestors. So when you are observing that heart problems or digestive upsets run in your family, it could be due to some trauma in the family line before you were born. You can do energy work to transform the energies of such traumas that are affecting you, and it can positively effect your health.

Your own past lives can also affect your present health. Allergies and sensitivities often seem to stem from trauma in a past life. Transform the energy of that trauma, and the allergy can go away. When we worked with clients, we saw many cases where lifelong food allergies were eliminated by clearing the past life energy that caused it. In one case, the allergy was strong enough to cause anaphylactic shock, but the client no longer reacted to that food after the clearing. In a later chapter, we discuss how you can use dowsing to discover about past lives and clear them to relieve allergies.

Genetics & Epigenetics

EVEN DOCTORS WILL TELL you that genes determine your health. This is largely false, and it is an outmoded belief that is only slowly being replaced with a more accurate and dynamic view of genes and health, so you need to educate yourself enough not to be trapped in the faulty belief that you can't change your genes if they are 'bad'.

Many years ago, science didn't know the truth about genes, and even now, there is still much to learn, but what has become obvious, yet still hasn't trickled down to the public, is that genes can be turned on or off. Just because you have a 'bad' gene doesn't mean it will be expressed, i.e., turned on.

Our knowledge of biochemistry, for example, (which explains a lot about physiology and health) is said to double every five years. Our knowledge of human biology in general is probably increasing at the same crazy rate. What this means is that when I got my Biology degrees in the 1970s, we only knew a fraction of what we now know. The truly mind-boggling bit is that it has been said that we only know about 5% of what there is to know, even now! The implications of this are nothing short of astonishing. What this means is we really don't know much about health and human biology at all.

The science of epigenetics is a fascinating topic, because it aligns with what we have always believed; that you are not condemned by your genetic heritage. You are a powerful creator and can neutralize or change things that appear to be detrimental. Many factors affect gene expression. Your diet, the energies in your environment and what you think all have an effect. By creating a healthy lifestyle and outlook, you can avoid expressing ill health, even if you carry a 'bad' gene, and that's because of epigenetics.

Think of it this way. For decades, there have been tons of campaigns about the evils of smoking and how it causes cancer. Many smokers have died of lung cancer. Yet some lifelong smokers never have lung illnesses of any kind. Just as not all smokers get cancer, not all 'bad' genes are 'turned on' or expressed. You have far more control than you think because of epigenetic factors.

Dowsing will help you make good health choices that leverage the positive effects of epigenetics and help you avoid the negative ones. Leveraging epigenetic factors is all about creating a healthy energetic and physical environment for your body, which means having a good diet, detoxing as needed, keeping your space clear and transforming negative beliefs and programs. There isn't a specific section on this topic, as it is affected by all your choices. Just be aware that you are not a prisoner of genetics.

Since any physical symptom is a reflection of an energy, it does seem reasonable that if you can inherit trauma from parents or grandparents, that trauma energy can lead to a pattern of ill health. It makes you wonder how often the perceived family tendency for a certain ailment could simply be a sign of inherited trauma coded into genes or imprinted in the subtle energy body somehow. When you have a symptom or condition that you see in one or both of your parents, or in a grandparent, it would be wise to dowse and determine if inherited trauma energy is responsible in part or completely for that health issue.

You can see that there are many contributing factors to good or ill health that are not physical, and if you wish to create good health, you would be wise to be aware of them and explore them using dowsing.

∼

Environmental Effects

YOUR ENVIRONMENT HAS a huge effect on your health, so you need to pay attention to it. There are physical elements in your environment, like toxins, that are detrimental to health. Pesticides in your food, contaminants in your water and chemtrails in the sky are examples. You can use dowsing to determine how much of an effect various aspects of your physical environment are having on your health.

Energies are invisible, and some can be just as noxious as physical toxins. You may be aware of the dangers of manmade EMFs (electromagnetic frequencies) from your microwave, smart phone (or smart anything) and wifi. We cannot emphasize enough how detrimental non-native EMFs are to your health, and unfortunately, it is next to impossible to protect yourself from them. The best thing to do is to limit exposure as much as possible.

Other noxious energies, like underground water and negative lines of energy, can only be found by dowsing. In addition to the above environmental effects, there are also things like entities, curses and alien energies that might be affecting your health.

Scientific studies have proven a correlation between geopathic energies (noxious earth energies) and the occurrence of cancer and other detrimental physiological changes. We have seen not only cancer, but other mental and physical health problems that were caused by other types of energies in the environment.

Your home and work space, where you spend the most time, have the greatest effect on your health. It is vital to have safe space to sleep and work (especially if you sit at a desk all day). Space clearing is a technique for harmonizing the energy of a space to transform detrimental energy to beneficial. This book is not about space clearing, but we do have two books on the topic, which you can see at Sixth Sense Books (see the Resources section for a link), or you can hire a professional to help you.

You can use dowsing to determine what noxious energies are at home or work and how intense they are, plus you can use it to find out how best to transform those energies. See the section on 'Environmental Energies' in the 'Dowsing Protocols' chapter for details.

Your environment has as great or a greater impact on your health than what you eat, so please don't ignore it.

Diet, Nutrition & Toxicity

ONE OF THE most significant physical environmental effects on your health relates to the surfaces that represent the point of contact between you and the outside world. Your skin is your largest organ, and it covers the outside of your body and protects you from detrimental factors in your environment, even while it interacts as Nature designed to create optimal health for you. Another surface that represents an interface between the outside world and your body is your gut lining. While technically it is inside of your body, it really is an outside surface that is designed not only to extract nutrients from your environment via your diet, but also to protect you from detrimental outside influences.

Both your skin and your gut have unique microbiota (collections of microorganisms) to help with this process. Anything that imbalances or harms the microorganisms can lead to ill health. Science is only now beginning to delve into the brain-gut axis and how important a balanced gut microbiota is. Antibiotics are a threat to the health of your gut microbiota, while chemically-laden personal care products are harmful to your skin microorganisms. These surfaces are your first line of defense for good health and require proper care.

Skin: Your Interface With The Outside World

We won't go into much detail about skin, but we urge you to recognize that personal care products, from shampoos to cosmetics, moisturizers and sunscreens can have ingredients that harm your skin and the microorganisms that dwell there. The more natural the products you use for personal care, the better. Coloring your hair and using tanning liquids introduce toxins that can have deleterious effects on your skin.

Another skin issue is the effects of non-native EMFs. Your skin cells are designed to pick up natural EMFs from the sun to help you be healthy, and non-native EMFs have been shown to pose a hazard to health in general, but to skin health in particular.

You don't need to be a dowser to choose to eliminate all toxins and chemicals from your environment and to reduce EMF exposure. Doing these things will improve your health. As a dowser, you can measure the actual effects on your health of these various factors as well as choose safer and healthier products.

The lining of your gut also demands the same level of protection, since when it becomes inflamed or imbalanced, it cannot do its job and keep you healthy. Eliminating toxins from your diet is the first step to creating a healthy gut. Again, you don't have to be a dowser to make healthy, common sense choices that will support gut health, but being a dowser will help you fine tune your eating regimen and repair gut damage.

Diet & Nutrition

Though diet and nutrition get a lot of attention as affecting your health, they are far from the only factors you need to address, and maybe not even the first to look at, but they are among the easiest to control. Just bear in mind that your beliefs and thoughts have a greater effect on your health than what you eat does, so don't focus only on food when trying to create better health.

The food and water you ingest are meant to nourish your body. The old saying "You are what you eat" has evolved into "You are what you absorb from what you eat", and that is more accurate, but still far from the complete picture. Yet, it's a good starting point.

Your digestive system is vitally important to your health. It affects not only things you might expect, like energy level and strength, but also your brain, your mood, and many other key activities. If you are not as healthy as you would like to be, a good starting point is to balance and optimize your digestion, even if you are not having obvious digestive issues.

If you are wanting to be a more healthy weight, it's fine to adjust your diet and exercise, but definitely study the environmental energy, genetics and beliefs sections, as they are even more fundamental to achieving your goals.

You are an individual. There is no one diet or nutritional plan that is perfect for everyone, so you need to experiment and study until you find the right one for you. Dowsing is useful for helping you streamline this process.

Water

Your body is made up mostly of water, so it makes sense that you should ingest plenty of pure water, yet most people live in a dehydrated condition and drink soda, coffee and alcoholic beverages instead. You can't substitute those for water. Most of them have negative health effects and tend to dehydrate you. If you want optimal health, switch to pure water.

Tap water is a convenience if you don't have well water, but it is not pure. I can remember as a child hating to drink water, because all we had was tap water, as we lived in the DC suburbs. Some years ago, my sister, who lived in Utah, commented that her dog didn't drink much water. I was standing in her kitchen at the time, and the area was full of bottled water. I asked her if the bottled water was for the dog as well as the humans. She said she just gave him tap water. I dumped his water bowl and filled it with bottled water, and when I put it on the floor, he drank half the bowl. I don't know if she gave him bottled water after that, but it proved my point. Tap water has things in it that you can smell and taste; children and animals are especially sensitive and will allow themselves to become dehydrated rather than drink tainted water.

There are filters and filter pitchers for purifying tap water, and you can dowse the best ones for your needs. There are also systems that filter your water, but do your due diligence. For example, some sources claim R/O (reverse osmosis) water is bad, because it is too pure and leaches minerals from your body.

Bottled water has the negative side effect of shedding plasticizers, which I get a reaction to, and if you are sensitive, you may want to avoid water from certain types of plastic containers. In addition, water that sits around will pick up energies from the location it's in, and those energies, if noxious, can be detrimental to your health.

If you are able to power intention (and most are not), you can transform the energy of water to beneficial using symbols, colors or some other type of physical 'anchor' for your intention. Such intentions often require frequent refreshing, but they can work if you have learned how to power intention.

You can use dowsing to check the purity of your water, decide on the best filtering system or figure out the most effective way to transform the energies to beneficial for you and your family.

There are sample dowsing questions about water in the 'Dowsing Protocols' chapter.

Food

Your body is unique, and the best diet for you (diet meaning regular eating plan) may differ from what is best for others, but there are some things that are just plain bad for everyone. You don't need dowsing to discover that. Sugar, processed foods, white flour and preservatives in general should be avoided. Not only do they lack what you need to be healthy, they are basically treated as toxins by the body. Sugar is also addictive. Basically, the typical American/modern processed food diet is unhealthy. It goes without saying that pesticides and GMOs are not natural, and the human body has not had time to evolve methods to deal with them. If you ingest such things, you are a guinea pig in an uncontrolled experiment.

Once you get the junk out of your diet, you may wonder what overall eating plan will work best for you. There are so many choices, you may find it confusing. You can take your personal preferences into account to some extent, but be aware that our bodies get addicted to eating what isn't good for us, and so just because you crave something doesn't mean you should eat it. For example, in nature, fat and sugars are rare, and many natural fats and sugars are healthy in small amounts. In modern society, you can get as much sugar or fat as you like, but it isn't the healthy kind. Your body isn't really craving Oreo cookies or french fries; it's programmed to take advantage of fats and sugar when they are available.

Constant hunger can be a sign of a nutrient-poor diet. Your body knows what it needs, and if you aren't getting it in your food, it will try to get you to keep eating, in hopes that you will eventually get the minerals, vitamins and enzymes you lack.

Craving a particular substance can be a sign of imbalance or dis-ease. An example is salt craving can be a sign of adrenal fatigue. Just eating potato chips isn't going to restore your adrenals to proper function. So you have to use your judgment, and dowsing is a great tool to help you discover the cause of your craving.

Humans evolved to be omnivores, which means your body is designed to eat just about anything natural: plants, animals, fruits, insects, nuts and seeds. In general, your body is designed to eat a lot of plant material of all colors. Eat the rainbow and avoid white and brown foods (potatoes, rice, other grains), and eat unprocessed foods, and you will go a long way towards healing yourself.

You may have some allergies and sensitivities, and avoiding foods that trigger those reactions until you can balance your system is a good idea. See the section on that subject in the 'Dowsing Protocols' chapter for details on how to use dowsing to help resolve allergies.

See also the section on diets in 'Dowsing Protocols' for details on dowsing the best diet for your needs. Be aware that in this book, we do not regard diets that are aimed at losing weight as good vehicles for your health. Your goal should be to discover an eating plan you can live with that meets your health and fitness goals and stick with it. Your weight will harmonize to whatever is best for you without focusing on it if you find the right eating plan and attend to some of the other factors we mention in this chapter.

In theory, the paleo/primal eating plan is the most geared to our evolutionary biology, but you'll notice with Paleo, you get 'cheating' as you do in all plans, and that cheating can defeat the purpose. Too many people eat a ton of red meat and meat in general on the Paleo diet, and that does not mimic what we were designed to eat. Meat should not be a big portion of your diet, especially red meat. To accommodate your body's biology, you should eat seasonal foods in the proportions they are found in Nature, eat more unprocessed foods and eat more foods that would have been easier to acquire in Nature with less energy output.

On the other end of the spectrum of diets, you have the vegetarian and vegan lifestyle choice, which does not align with your human biology as an omnivore. If you choose to be a vegetarian, you are going against evolution, and you need to supplement to avoid certain deficiencies that are caused by eschewing meat as a source of protein. Fat soluble vitamins like K2 are an important example of animal-based nutrition that vegetarians who won't eat dairy or eggs will completely miss out on.

Vegetables are good for you, but the 'cheating' on vegetarian diets is to eat too many starches and processed vegetarian foods, which have poor food value. When you combine the deficiencies and the cheats, you can end up with long term health issues on a diet that eliminates meat proteins. However, if you eat unprocessed vegetables and fruits in a good balance, and you supplement properly, you can probably be healthy on this kind of a diet.

Fad diets aimed at weight loss are not worth considering in our opinion. If you have excess weight, you need to adopt a different lifestyle, and you need to address more than just what you eat and how you exercise. The next sections will help give you some things to think about. Your goals are more realistic if you select an eating plan you like that you can live with that helps you reach your health goals. In our opinion, your thoughts, beliefs and even factors like non-native EMFs have more of an effect on weight than diet and exercise. If you have excess weight, you must consider those factors as well if you want permanent improvement.

There are an infinite variety of diets and eating plans, and most of them have a kernel of truth, but all of them have down sides and 'cheating' occurs that nullifies the good effects. We suggest you research diets and try to pick one that is truly based on human evolutionary biology rather than political, religious or other bias. It should be noted that diets that were once touted as optimal for athletes have now been found in many cases to lead to premature death and heart disease. Just because a diet is in vogue does not mean it is healthy for you.

In summary, there is no perfect diet for everyone, and dowsing will help you evaluate what is best for you and your health goals. Always look at long term effects, and don't be afraid to make changes, because your body is always changing, as is your environment. Don't settle on one diet and stick with it forever; use your dowsing to check in from time to time and make adjustments as needed.

Sleep

SLEEP IS UNDERVALUED but vital to health. During sleep, your body repairs and restores itself. If your circadian rhythms are off or your diet is bad or your cortisol levels are upside down, sleep becomes a problem, and getting good sleep is the foundation of maintaining good health and restoring and rebalancing when you have ill health. It is no surprise that sleep deprivation is one of the oldest forms of torture.

Our culture tends to put us in rational mind overdrive, as if thinking is the solution to all our problems. Too often, you go to bed and want to think about how to solve whatever is stressing you. Bedtime is not the time to think. It's the time to sleep.

Constant stress, even low level stress, can cause your cortisol levels to reverse from their normal pattern, causing you to have problems waking up in the morning and going to sleep at night. Cortisol imbalance due to stress is usually a sign of adrenal challenges. It is important to eliminate unnecessary stress and to find constructive ways of dealing with stress you cannot avoid. Relaxation methods and meditation are very helpful in this regard, as is renouncing the extra responsibilities you sometimes pile on yourself.

Your diet can also disrupt your sleep. Caffeine, alcohol and sugars and starches, when ingested in the evening, will cause a sugar spike that will wake you up. Try not to snack in the evenings or eat your dinner too late.

Your circadian rhythms are controlled by the light from the sun. Your eyes are designed to interpret what time of day it is by the quality of light they detect. Daytime light means be awake, sunset means time to prepare for sleep. The use of sunglasses, electric lights after dark and computer screens of all kinds disrupt your body's ability to know what time of day it is. Your eyes need to be in natural light to set your rhythms.

We have stopped using sunglasses except in extreme driving conditions for safety. We don't use electric lights after dark; instead, we use oil lanterns. And we use blue blocker glasses or programs to reduce blue light when looking at any kind of computer screen, and we limit as much as possible, any type of screen-staring activity. We watch TV one night a week and even write first drafts of our books longhand to avoid messing with our biological clocks.

Anything you can do to improve the quality of sleep you have and get the right amount will contribute to healing and overall good health.

Stress

ENOUGH HAS BEEN WRITTEN about the effects of stress on health that everyone is aware of it, but how often do we tell ourselves we aren't stressed when we are, or that we just can't make changes that will reduce stress? A key to your health is being really honest with yourself and eliminating all sources of unnecessary stress from your life.

If you are in a relationship or a job that gives you constant stress, get out. Don't make excuses for staying, because money or reputation are no substitute for being healthy and alive. Don't make other people your excuse for staying in a stressful situation, either. Your kids won't appreciate your staying with an abusive spouse, and they'll just learn bad habits. Your aging parents may be your responsibility, but you have a right to do things to help you reduce the stress of caring for them. Don't always make yourself a martyr or the only responsible person in your family. Let others, no, demand that others help.

If you are truly in a situation that you believe you have no choice about leaving, then at the very least, find ways to give yourself mental health time every day, even if it's only 15 minutes. Read a book, soak in a bubble bath, meditate, do tai chi or yoga, tap on your emotions, work in your garden, walk your dog. Any of those activities can recharge your batteries if you do them from love and not because they are another chore on your already long list.

It's up to you to assess and reduce your stress. Modern living puts a lot of burdens on us, and it's up to us to lay them down and lighten our loads as much as possible. Don't do things out of obligation or because someone expects it. Do things you want to do. And if your life is full of things you don't want to do, then take steps to change your beliefs, because they are causing you problems. It isn't always easy, but if you commit to it, you can create the life you want. And it will help heal your body, mind and spirit.

Summary

THIS CHAPTER IS A VERY important one, because it presents you with a new, broader way of looking at health. You probably already knew that the subtle energy body exists, and that ill health begins there. But maybe you were not aware of how many factors affect physical health: things like environmental energies, beliefs, past lives and epigenetic factors going back for generations.

Our goal is to help you fine tune your outlook on health so that instead of focusing only on diet, supplements and remedies, you step back and look at the big picture of health and all that contributes to it, and you not only pay attention to those factors, you give them as much or more attention than you do the conventionally accepted things like diet, exercise and therapies.

It has taken us many years of studying, reading, working with clients and for our own personal healing to understand how many things contribute to health, and that many of those things are unconventional, but very powerful. If you accept this perspective and begin to educate yourself in how to deal with these strange nonphysical factors, you will see improvement in your health and well-being.

Much of this has its origin in the belief that we co-create our reality, and that everything we see 'out there' is a reflection of our own personal energy. We advise you to study the Law of Attraction, as it is very helpful for those who wish to express good health and well-being. Our understanding of all the factors that contribute to health is constantly evolving, so this chapter is not the last word, just our most recent understanding of a very complex subject. We encourage you to keep fine-tuning your perspective on health, as we are.

5

DOWSING ACCURATELY

Introduction

You need to be a good dowser to dowse for health. This chapter is merely a refresher to remind you of some of the key aspects of good dowsing technique that can impact your dowsing accuracy.

If you are confident about your dowsing, you can skip this chapter, but most people will be able to mine at least one dowsing gem from this refresher.

~

The Dowsing State

THE DOWSING state is an altered state that a dowser enters into in order to receive the answer to her question. Studies have shown that the dowsing state has measurably different brain waves from a normal resting state. If you are not in a dowsing state, you are not dowsing. It's that simple. You can still get a 'yes' or 'no' answer to your dowsing question, but it will be provided by your rational mind rather than via dowsing.

Health dowsing can be very trivial or it can be a matter of life or death. Being able to dowse accurately depends on your being able to enter that hard-to-describe state of mind that will allow the correct answer to your question to come to you.

Some of the things that prevent you from attaining a dowsing state are:

- Your need to be right
- Distractions (especially for newbies)
- A strong rational faculty
- An inability to release control
- Fear of a 'wrong' answer and what it means
- Misunderstanding dowsing technique

Practice and studying proper technique allow you to master the dowsing state. It can be described as a state in which you are focused on only one thing: the dowsing question, and you are completely detached about what the answer will be, although you are curious as to what it is.

Detachment & Fear

WITH RESPECT TO HEALTH DOWSING, detachment is a critical requirement for accuracy, yet when you are dowsing important health questions, fear of the answer may prevent you from being detached. How do you learn detachment?

Detachment must be learned through practice, and lots of it. It's easy to be detached when you aren't concerned about the answer, but if you are asking if your dog has cancer or that headache you have is a brain tumor, being detached will be quite a challenge. Yet it is precisely at times like that when you need detachment.

Don't wait until you are health dowsing about life or death issues to learn detachment. Start by dowsing questions that you are just curious about, then graduate to questions for which you might prefer a certain answer, and practice staying simply curious as to what the answer will be. When you don't have that clenched feeling of fear, move on to slightly more challenging questions.

You can tell if you are afraid. When you are not detached, you may tense or clench part of your body as if to ward off the blow of an unwanted answer. You may hold your breath.

Practice being relaxed, breathing normally and just being curious whenever you dowse. If you find that you are not detached, don't dowse. Your answer more than likely will be wrong.

When someone is not detached, the subconscious knows the answer that is coming, and often, your body's polarity will flip to give you the desired answer instead of the correct answer. Checking your polarity before, during and after a tough dowsing session will detect polarity reversal that comes as a result of fear or strong desire for a certain question. Understanding polarity, what it is and how to correct it is covered in any good dowsing course.

∽

Ask The Right Question

A GOOD DOWSING question yields a reliable answer. A poor question is a waste of time. A good dowsing question is usually long and detailed, and it includes who, what, where, when, how and why, as appropriate.

The tendency not to formulate a detailed question probably stems from the perception of dowsing as a psychic activity rather than a natural skill. Psychics seem to snatch answers out of the air with ease, and those who wish to have psychic powers and believe dowsing is such will not see the need to spend time on a clearly defined question, thinking that as long as they can get an answer, it must be true. Some people even seem to regard dowsing as channeling, which it is not. When you are dowsing, you are not asking some advanced being a question. Dowsing is a skill for getting answers via focused intuition, and the validity of those answers depends in large part on asking clear questions.

We have a compendium of good dowsing questions in our book *Ask The Right Question*, which can be seen on our Sixth Sense Books website. We have copied the health section of that book into this one for you as a bonus, and you can see them at the end of the book.

Take time to craft a detailed and specific dowsing question. Don't rush to the dowsing as if that's the most important part.

Avoid vague words like 'good' and 'highest good' in your question, instead using your specific, measurable health goals instead. Using vague terms expecting someone else will sort it out for you, even a higher power, is trying to take a short cut in the dowsing process, and it doesn't help you master dowsing.

Never assume the meaning of a word. Your subconscious might have a different definition for 'better' or 'significant' than your conscious mind does. Assumptions lead to bad answers. Define terms carefully, even ones you think are self-evident.

Write the question down. Write your answer down. Later on, go back and confirm if the answer was correct, if possible. If it was wrong, look at the question and try to figure out how the answer you got was right *for that question*. This is an exercise we have used to improve our dowsing questions. As you examine the question, you will note vague or ambiguous words and missing elements you wouldn't recall if you hadn't written the question down. This will help you make better dowsing questions.

No one is a great dowser at first. It takes time and a lot of practice to master dowsing. Be patient with yourself and don't worry about mistakes, as you can learn a lot from them.

Getting Help

WE'VE POINTED out that health dowsing sometimes is about life or death issues, whether you want to know if it's time to euthanize your dog or if you have lung cancer. Since no dowser is 100% accurate, when you are dowsing serious issues, it is vital that you get a second and even a third opinion before taking action.

A dowsing buddy can be a real asset. If you learn dowsing with a friend or family member, and you support each other and practice a lot, then you can ask each other to dowse important questions. You can do blind dowsing if you prefer, meaning ask the person to dowse a yes/no question, but don't tell them what it is. Hold it in your mind or write it on a piece of paper and ask them to dowse that question.

A lot of folks don't have a dowsing buddy, and their fallback position is to dowse the same question more than once. Invariably, when they do that, they get conflicting answers to the same question. This is because your subconscious only wants you to ask a question once. Asking it more than once sounds like you want another answer, or you don't trust your dowsing. In either case, dowsing again is simply not a good idea.

If you don't have a dowsing buddy, what you can do is form slightly different questions about various aspects of the same topic and note if they all seem to point to the same answer. The questions must be different enough that they give different information on that topic. You then compare the answers to see if they all make sense. This is not a substitute for having a second or third opinion, but it is useful at times.

If you absolutely can't get another dowser of similar or better accuracy to dowse on your subject, then you can use other outside sources to confirm your answers in other ways. A lab test might confirm the dowsing answer you got. Or the vet might say he feels it's time for your dog to be put to sleep. Another expert opinion or test results that support your dowsing may be substituted for a second dowsing opinion.

Practice Refining Your Technique

IF YOU WANT to be an accurate dowser, you need to use it as often as possible. Not only have both of us dowsed almost daily for ourselves for years, we also worked many hours a week dowsing for clients. This gave us a very fast learning curve covering a wide variety of subjects that won't be available to most dowsers.

If you are working full time and have a family, it may be challenging to carve out time for your dowsing, but you need to commit to it if you want to be accurate. Read lots of books, take lots of classes, practice dowsing things that will improve your life.

About 80% of what you dowse about should be tangible target dowsing, things you can confirm. By that, I don't mean coin tosses or card suits. That is a waste of time, because it tries to make a game or test of dowsing.

Dowsing is meant to be used to help make your life better, to give you answers you want to get, but can't get rationally. Dowse everyday subjects that fit this description. Our book *101 Amazing Things You Can Do With Dowsing* will give you plenty of examples, along with good dowsing questions. The digital version is free at all retailers.

For the other 20% of your dowsing, it's ok to dowse things that interest you that you cannot confirm in any way, but you will not become a good dowser unless you are able to make mistakes and figure out how to improve your technique, so try hard to make 80% of your dowsing tangible target dowsing. Making mistakes teaches you about detachment, good questions and the dowsing state more than anything we can tell you in a book. If you have never made a mistake dowsing, you probably haven't been dowsing. If you are unwilling to examine your mistakes and think about how to improve your dowsing, you are missing a great opportunity. And if you have never been surprised by a dowsing answer, you definitely have not been dowsing, because the answers are not always what one expects.

Mastery takes time. Don't be in a rush. Let yourself learn and grow. Learn from your mistakes. If you keep at it, you will master dowsing.

~

Confirming Results

As we mentioned in the 'Getting Help' section earlier, you can't always confirm your results when you are health dowsing, but if you make an effort to do so whenever you can, it is a great way of gaining confidence and also gives you a chance to improve your technique.

We suggest that for any important dowsing, you write down your question, date it and make notes about your state of mind and goals at the time. Then, give yourself time to see the results, and if they are not what you expected, look at your question to see how you can improve it by making it more detailed, more specific and by using clearer words, or at least by defining your terms better. You can also ask yourself how your answer could have been true for the question as it was worded, which will help you to improve your future questions.

Obviously, any condition for which you get lab tests can confirm your dowsing results. If you are trying to improve your liver enzymes, heal anemia or balance your immune system, a simple blood test can show whether or not the program you adopted has succeeded, and how much. Likewise for any test that supposedly shows a disease condition is present or not. (We urge you to consider lab tests as merely a snapshot of your condition at the moment of the test. Do not identify with a condition, as that makes it harder to change.)

Other results may be less subject to specific proof, but subjective proof may be adequate. If you are working to improve your energy level, you can tell if you have succeeded, especially if you keep a diary where you note your energy level on a daily basis by using a number scale or writing what you were capable of doing.

Noting the date you started a program is wise, because you can dowse how long before you reach a certain goal or how long it will be until you see significant results (making sure you define 'significant' clearly). Then when the time is up, evaluate your progress.

Another trick you can use is if you aren't doing lab tests, assign a number on a scale of 0 to 10 for your level of energy, intensity of pain or other symptom. Note it in your journal, giving either the highest level or an average for the day. Make notes about the frequency and duration of a symptom as well. Over time, you should see changes for the better if your program is working.

Most health changes won't happen overnight, but of course, any that do are confirmation that what you did worked.

If you don't get confirmation that your dowsing was correct, don't be discouraged. There may be more than one factor at work, and you may need to work on something else to get your desired results. Or perhaps your dowsing technique needs some refinement. By examining your results, you are more likely to find ways to improve your dowsing, and you will also build your confidence.

6

DOWSING TECHNIQUES

Introduction

What follows are some valuable dowsing techniques that health dowsers use often. Most of these are taught in any good intermediate or advanced dowsing course, but maybe you haven't learned them all. If you have, this will be a good refresher for how to apply them in health dowsing. If this is new information to you, please practice it until you feel confident before using the techniques in life or death situations.

Scales

SCALES ARE numerical ways of assigning value to a subject. The two most common scales we use in health dowsing are 0 to 10 and +10 to -10. "But wait", you're thinking, "isn't dowsing about getting yes or no answers?" Indeed it is. And when you use a scale, you are asking what number is closest to the answer. In a sense, you are asking, "Is the answer 0? 1? 2?" and so on until you get a 'yes'.

Using a scale is far more valuable than just a simple yes/no answer. If you are trying to pick the best vitamin C supplement out of 12 on the shelf in your favorite health food store, you will probably get 'yes' for too many of them to be useful. But if you use a scale, then you can buy the one that gives you a 10 on a scale of 0-10. Or you might even find out that none of them is a 10. And if you get more than one 10, you can make your question more detailed until you get a clear winner.

The 0-10 scale is valuable for measuring intensity, accuracy, how strong side effects will be and other things that can go from nothing to very strong. An example would be if you ask the question, "On a scale of 0 to 10, with 0 being none and 10 being the worst it could be, what is the level of side effects I will experience if I take this drug as prescribed for 30 days?" For this type of question, anything over a 3 would give me cause to rethink taking the drug, because I have observed after lots of dowsing that a 3 is a pretty unpleasant reaction for me, but each person is unique. You might find that you're OK with anything below a 5.

You can see how beneficial a treatment or supplement will be for a given condition by using the same scale. If you want to cure a vitamin deficiency you have been shown to have, you can ask how beneficial a certain product taken as directed will be for restoring the balance in your body of that vitamin within a certain time period (or even for a certain price). In that case, anything that gives 8 or higher in our opinion is worth buying.

The +10 to -10 scale is used when you are asking about something that can be either beneficial, neutral or detrimental. The most important question we use this scale for is when we ask the long term level in effects (overall results) on our health and well-being of the process that is causing a particular symptom we are now experiencing. We'll go into more detail on that later. Another example is when you set aside prejudice and ask what the overall results will be for a given goal if you take a certain drug, get a recommended surgery or even go to a doctor for a consultation. This scale is also useful in measuring the overall energy in your home and how it affects your health, or for evaluating your diet or exercise program for your goals.

You can use both the 0-10 or +10 to -10 scales for the same thing in some cases. It's just a matter of preference. Pick whichever you feel will give you the most meaningful information for your purpose.

Scales can be used whether you are dowsing with a pendulum or with no tool at all. You can use scales by imagining them in your head or by using a chart or diagram. You must include the scale in the question, while also defining what at least some of the numbers mean to you, as in 0 means no effect, 10 means you die.

The 0-10 scale is most often shown as a line with 0 at one end, and 10 at the other, with the numbers marked in between at even intervals.

For the +10 to -10 scale, the most common chart resembles a protractor with -10 at the lower left of the semicircle and +10 at the lower right point of the half-circle, with 0 being the middle top of the curve, perpendicular to the horizontal line that forms the base. (Now don't you wish you'd paid attention in high school math?) The scales can also just be visualized on the table in front of you.

Really, though, you don't need a chart or visual aid to use scales. In fact, we never do anymore. If you are new to using scales, you can say the numbers slowly until you get a 'yes' for the correct one, as in, 0, 1, 2, 3, 4, and so on. If you want to be quicker, you can ask if the answer is 8 or greater, or if it is a negative number (if you are using the +10 to -10 scale). Then you can home in and get the actual number without having to say every single one.

You won't be able to dive deep into health dowsing if you don't use scales, so practice using them on everyday dowsing subjects and get used to them, because they give you a lot more information than a simple 'yes' or 'no'.

There is another use of scales that is worth discussing here. Bearing in mind that no dowser is 100% accurate, that you can be attached to a certain answer and that sometimes it's hard to form a good question, you might wish to have a way to determine if the answer you obtained when dowsing is correct, especially if it is an important question. While it seems counterintuitive to suggest this, I have found that I can test the accuracy of an answer using a 0 to 10 scale immediately after I dowse, and if I get less than a 10, it causes me to rethink the situation. In other words, I don't trust the answer if I don't get a 10. I try to think of a new dowsing approach to the problem. (I have found another counterintuitive use of dowsing, which is when my polarity is reversed, and I ask if my polarity is reversed, I get an accurate answer, which makes no sense at all if my polarity is reversed. But it works for me, so I don't worry about it.)

Level In Effects

IN THE PREVIOUS SECTION, we discussed two scales which are very useful to health dowsers. When you ask your dowsing question, you may well include the phrase 'level in effects' when you are asking how strong or weak, how good or bad, how useful or worthless and how detrimental or beneficial something is for your health or well-being. The phrase is so versatile, you will find yourself using it when dowsing about everything, including finances, relationships, career and everyday dowsing!

If you are using a yes/no question, you don't need to look at level in effects, but when you go to scales and inspect a deeper level with more detail, the phrase 'level in effects' is a handy generalization that helps tie all your dowsing together, because you will use it over and over and begin to get a feel for what the numbers are trying to tell you.

Each person is different, and you should look for patterns in your dowsing as you get answers so that you can predict what cutoff is best for your needs.

For example, I have found that if I am dowsing side effects of a supplement, therapy or drug, anything larger than a 3 on a scale of 0 to 10 means I should find a substitute. When something tests 0, 1, 2 or 3, I can handle the side effects, though 3 is not pleasant.

Another example is that when we are dowsing for overall level in effects of a treatment or drug or supplement, we want to see a number that is 8 or higher before we invest money in it. We have seen the pattern that for us, anything less than an 8 might be disappointing for our goals.

The beauty of using scales is that they give you so much more detail. You can tell a strong 'yes' from a weak 'yes'. This is vital when you are considering investing money or getting surgery or taking a drug.

'Level in effects' is just a fancy way of asking what the outcome would be on the numerical scale you are using.

～

Chart & List Dowsing

IF YOU HAVE HAD a good course in dowsing, you should know how to dowse using lists and charts. Charts are very popular for pendulum dowsing, while lists can be used for deviceless dowsing. There are whole books of charts for dowsing about health, and good ones are an excellent starting point in your health journey, especially if you are not well-trained in human biology.

A chart basically lists all the possible answers to a question along with 'other' so that you can dowse for the answer. If you get 'other', then you have to research and dowse some more, because that means the answer is not on that chart. We haven't used charts for years now, partly because we don't use tools to dowse very often, but beginners find them very helpful.

If you are a deviceless dowser like us, and you don't use tools, then list dowsing may be the answer for you. A list is basically the same as a chart, because the list has all the possible answers plus 'other' that you can dowse using a deviceless technique like blink dowsing or finger dowsing. If you have had a course in dowsing, it should have covered a few of the many deviceless methods, and we advise you to master one or two at least.

You can quickly dowse a list of possibilities to find your answer, but you need to know what the possibilities are in order to make the list. This is where having some knowledge of health is important. If you don't know what therapies or remedies are used for liver problems, how can you make a list to dowse?

We advise you to keep a dowsing journal, and it is helpful to have a list of therapies and remedies and causes of problems that you add to over time.

Lists and charts are particularly useful for choosing therapies, supplements, remedies and finding causes of problems, because there are usually a number of options, and you want to find the best one.

Combining Dowsing & Healing

DOWSING IS NOT A HEALING METHOD. Some confuse pendulum dowsing with pendulum healing, because pendulum healing also uses a pendulum. Many activities use a pendulum that are not dowsing. Hypnosis and pendulum healing are not dowsing. Don't think that anything done with a pendulum is dowsing. It is not.

Dowsing is actually more powerful than a healing method, because it combines with any healing method. By using dowsing to get information about the cause of your problem and how to resolve it, you can get far better results than if you just throw a supplement or healing method at a symptom.

There are many wonderful healing methods you can learn. Some require a lot of work to master, while others are simple. You are unique and should choose to learn at least a few healing methods that resonate with you. If you pursue health dowsing diligently, you may find that as you change, you resonate more with another healing method. I started out with Reiki, and I still use it occasionally, but I also have used SRT (Spiritual Response Therapy), EFT (Emotional Freedom Technique), Senzar Clearing, Jin Shin Jyutsu, Toning, and crystals, symbols and color, to name a few. Nigel learned all of them and was also certified in Spiritual Healing. No healing method heals every problem, so it's good to have a number of tools in your tool kit. It takes time to accumulate this kind of experience, but it pays off.

You don't have to learn a healing method to be a health dowser. You can go to professionals if you have the money to do so. Just dowse what professional healing method will be the most help for your situation. In that case, you need a list of professionals who offer a variety of services whom you would be willing to consult.

There are remedies like supplements, herbs and essential oils that you can use to speed your healing process, but to use them wisely, you need to be educated about them. There are many books on these topics and plenty of experts who can guide you, so whether you intend to master a subject yourself or just want to consult a professional, health dowsing will be a useful tool in choosing your path.

7
DOWSING PROTOCOLS

Introduction

It would be great if there were 3 steps we could tell you to follow that would easily 'cure' whatever ails you. Unfortunately, health is a very complex subject, and you are a unique individual. What works for someone else may not work for you. Therefore, we can't give you an encyclopedia of 'cures' or even perfect dowsing protocols for a given dis-ease. Our goal is to provide you with the skill to improve your health using techniques that work for you, but you will have to take the journey one step at a time.

The uniqueness of your situation is the fundamental reason you need to take control of your health and learn health dowsing, because it puts you in charge by giving you customized advice. Becoming a masterful health dowser allows you to guide your health in the direction you want it to go. Granted, this is a departure from conventional medicine, which has a one-size-fits-all approach to health, but our experience has shown us that you can get better results when you acknowledge your uniqueness.

Whether you have a symptom or a diagnosis or no dis-ease at all, your goal is to improve your health. If you are taking a holistic approach, the protocols in this chapter will help you find the root cause of your issue or create the perfect regimen to support your health goals. If you are merely trying to find a therapy or test the side effects of a recommended drug, you can use the appropriate protocols in this chapter for that purpose.

If you have a symptom but haven't been to a doctor, use the 'Good Or Bad?' protocol and then check out the 'Do You Need A Doctor?' test.

If you have a diagnosis and wish to determine a root cause, you can use the 'Finding Root Causes' protocol or just use the various other protocols in this chapter until you get answers that point you in a direction that feels right for your needs. There may be a number of contributing factors to your health challenge, and these protocols will help you uncover them.

If you are setting up a regimen for maintenance or prevention, read through the entire chapter, and then use dowsing to determine which protocol will be most useful to you at this time if you didn't get an obvious intuitive or rational hit. A scale is the best way to determine that. Here's a sample question:

On a scale of 0 to 10, with 10 meaning incredibly valuable for my health goals and 0 meaning no value, what value is _____protocol for me at this time?

You may know the condition that you want to address, but you may not at this time be aware of what the cause of the problem is, so you can dowse which protocol will guide you best in finding the cause of the symptom or condition that is bothering you. Here is a sample question:

On a scale of 0 to 10, with 10 meaning incredibly valuable for discovering the root cause of _____(describe your symptom without using a diagnostic term, that is, a disease name), what value is the _____protocol at this time?

Remember the path to health is not always a straight line, nor is it always smooth. But if you are clear about your goals, dowsing will guide you along the path that will be most beneficial for them.

These exercises will really show you how good a dowser you are. If you don't get surprised occasionally, you probably aren't dowsing accurately. If you feel fear when dowsing any of these protocols, you aren't adequately detached, and your answers will be incorrect. If you always get the answer you want to get, you probably are not dowsing. Be brutally honest with yourself and go back to improving your dowsing technique if you discover that you are having challenges like these.

In using these protocols, remember that we still know so little of what creates good or bad health, that we need to stay flexible in our thinking. If you have been alive long enough or watch trends, you know that what is thought of as great now may turn out to be totally rejected at some future date, and that what is seen as bad now may be adopted as healthy in the future. For example, the lipid hypothesis of heart disease has been proven to be wrong, even though it lingers in the conventional mentality. More and more people are seeing that fats of certain kinds aid good health, that cholesterol has an important role to play in your body and that many of the most common drugs being used today to prevent heart attacks are not only ineffective, but have bad side effects. Butter is in. Margarine is out.

Try to be open to seeing things in new ways, to reading and thinking critically about your most cherished assumptions and never just accept things based on what Science claims is right, right now. It will all change, because we know only a tiny bit of what we need in order to understand this beautiful and complex human body and how it works.

Our basic assumption we use at this time is natural is usually better, but that is based on our definition of natural and is just a starting point to give you a long view about health and to challenge your basic assumptions. The farther you step back to view health and the more open you are, the more prepared you will be to create good health, at least in our opinion.

Finally, these are not the only dowsing protocols you can use for health dowsing. They cover the most common health topics, but you may want to create your own protocols as you become more confident and experienced. You can use the principles in these protocols to create your own and take your health dowsing to an even more advanced level.

Is It Good Or Bad?

THIS PROTOCOL IS one of the first to turn to whenever you have a symptom that concerns you. Most people do not know about this protocol, because they make too many assumptions, and assumptions are almost always a mistake.

When you are dowsing, you should always 'back up' in terms of your perspective until you have removed your prejudices and preconceived notions from the equation. This helps you become more detached and also improves your dowsing accuracy. When you have used this protocol a few times, you will understand the value of it, and you will begin to see why a dowser should always back up for a wider perspective before creating a dowsing question.

If you have a minor symptom, most likely you will ignore it for at least a couple or three days, because minor issues seem to resolve themselves without a lot of care. However, if you have an acute symptom or you have a symptom that lasts more than 3 days, you probably want to look into it, because it is a message from your body.

Symptoms that get our attention are usually painful or at least uncomfortable. We don't tend to notice when our bodies perform perfectly, which is a shame. We only notice when our body malfunctions. Your symptom might be a headache that lasts for two days or a sharp pain somewhere or your knee is not working well or your stomach is unsettled.

Don't make any assumptions. Let's find out whether that symptom is a sign of something that in the long run is good or bad for you.

Step 1

Think about and describe the symptom or condition that is bothering you.

Step 2

Dowse whether the **root cause** of that symptom is good or bad for you. How could it be good? Well, if you just started a new exercise program or are learning tai chi, you might have some aches and pains, and they could be pretty disturbing. But if it's just your body getting toned up, in the long run, it's a good thing. You can support the process with heat or an essential oil combo or a topical product for sore muscles, but you don't have a disease, and you don't have anything to worry about.

On the other hand, a pain could be torn cartilage, a damaged muscle or inflammation, which is not part of a healing, detoxing or growth process. Trauma and dis-ease require a different type of support so that healing may occur. In other words, left alone, they are bad for you.

You can't always use your rational mind to figure out whether the cause of your symptom is positive or negative (like you could with the muscle soreness), so you'll need to dowse. We use a +10 to -10 scale for this purpose.

A negative number indicates an imbalance or dis-ease process that should be addressed to resolve the root cause, while a positive number means a beneficial process like a detox or a transformation like your muscles are getting stronger or you are releasing something that no longer serves you. If the process is positive, you can still ask how to support it to make it more comfortable.

This dowsing question is the one we always use whenever we can't tell what the cause of a symptom is using our rational minds. Not assuming that pain means illness is a departure from the typical Western view of health, which aims to eradicate all pain, regardless of cause, as if pain always means something bad. By dowsing this question, you acknowledge that sometimes, growth and progress are painful or uncomfortable, and you choose not to assume that every discomfort is bad.

We use the following question to determine how to judge a symptom:

On a +10 to -10 scale, with negative numbers meaning detrimental to me, what is the overall long-term level in effects on my health and well-being of the process that is causing_____ (name the symptom).

Note that we aren't the least interested in dowsing about the symptom. We already know that the symptom is a nuisance, and we'd like to get rid of it. All we care about is the root cause of the symptom and whether that cause is a beneficial or a detrimental process for our long-term health.

If you get a 0, that means neutral. If you get a positive number, the process that is causing the symptom is beneficial to you, with higher positive numbers being more so. For many years, we have used this question, and it has amazed us how often a very unpleasant symptom is part of a highly beneficial process. (This is more likely to be the case if you are actively doing things to improve your health.)

A positive number can mean you are detoxing, going through a release or some kind of transformation (changes in muscles during workout is an example of the latter). Usually, a beneficial process comes from an activity you have recently adopted, like a new workout program, a new supplement or a new type of energy work or therapy.

A negative number means you have some kind of imbalance or disease process, and it would be wise to address the root cause and resolve it so the symptom can go away. A high negative number means a very bad outcome if left untreated.

When you use this protocol, you will find that often, something that you might have thought was bad is actually beneficial for you in the long run. You will stop assuming that all pain is bad and that you must be afraid whenever you have discomfort. You will learn to take action to support positive processes to make them smoother and easier, and you will also get focused on treating the root cause of your symptom rather than simply erasing it.

If you get a -8 or worse, definitely get a second opinion from another good dowser or see your health care professional. If you get a -1 to -7, further dowsing to reveal a way to resolve the cause of the issue is going to be required. But first, use the 'Do You Need A Doctor?' protocol to see if you can handle the situation on your own. If so, check out the section later in this chapter on choosing modalities, remedies and therapies.

If you get a 0, you can ignore the symptom.

If you get a positive number, you can dowse further if you wish, in order to find a way to make the process easier and more comfortable for you (if that is possible).

∼

Do You Need A Doctor?

IN THIS SECTION, we will discuss what we regard as the single most important health dowsing question you can master, because if you can become accurate at answering this question, you will save yourself untold money and trouble, and you may even save a life. We have used this question often for ourselves and our pets, and we can confirm it's priceless, as you may recall from the earlier story about Nigel's mole.

The health dowsing question that we have used most often with the greatest benefit is, "Do I need a doctor?" (or a vet, if this is a pet problem).

Asking The Question

Now, it would be so nice if you could just dowse that simple question, but if you've been paying attention, you probably have guessed that you can't do that without some preparation. That particular question is too vague and too ill-defined to give you a good answer. Let's discuss why that is, as it's a good lesson in the importance of having goals and asking a specific question with clearly defined terms.

What does the question really mean? Especially, what does the word 'need' mean to you? Perhaps everyone in our culture consciously or subconsciously thinks they need a doctor for any health challenge. If you are one of them, asking this as a dowsing question will mostly yield a 'yes' answer, but it won't necessarily be an answer to the question you want to ask.

What you probably want to know includes some or all of the following factors:

- Can you afford what it is going to cost to consult with a professional in this situation? This is especially true these days for vet visits, which aren't covered by insurance.
- Is going to a doctor going to yield the outcome you want?
- Is going to the doctor going to give you faster, better results than trying to take care of this yourself using what you know?
- Will there be any negative side effects to consulting a doctor?
- Is this health situation so serious that you really would be wisest to see a professional as soon as possible?

You get the picture. You might have other factors that matter to you, such as the time you will have to take off from work to visit the doctor or vet.

Make a detailed list of your unique needs and preferences. Include the maximum budget you have to spend (if this is something that might cost money) and any other factor that matters to you. Then and only then will you be ready to find out if going to a doctor is best for your unique situation.

Programming Your Question

For very long and detailed questions, especially ones like this one, which are most often needed at times when you are under stress and having challenges about being detached, it is useful to have programmed yourself, or your dowsing system, however you want to regard it, so that you can use a short form of the question.

Having programmed a short question to mean something complex and more detailed allows you to ask the short question and get the answer to the longer one, which is very helpful in times of stress.

You can make the short form anything you like. You can even include words you normally wouldn't use, because you will have programmed their meaning in advance. So the key is to think about this carefully while you aren't in an emergency situation, define your goals and preferences, and then program the question. The question should be simple, like "Do I need a doctor/vet for this issue?" or "Should I see a doctor about this?" Use words that seem right to you.

You program the question using a simple statement of intention with good focus. You have made your list, and you make a statement out loud that is something like this:

When I ask the question "Should I see a doctor about this?", it means _____(insert your long, complex question here).

Your long question includes every factor that matters to you, and it will be unique for you. We can't give you one that will be perfect for your needs, and bear in mind that those can change over time. Your budget might change, your perception of what you can handle on your own might change, etc.

You get to decide if there are some factors that are more important than others, or if you are just seeking an overall answer to the entire list of factors.

Programming Your Answer

After you have programmed the short question to include all the factors on your list, you can program your answer in a number of ways. This is optional, but it will help you get a more reliable answer. Here are some examples.

Give me a 'yes' answer to the question "Should I see a doctor about this" if overall for my list of needs (you can state them if you like), consulting a doctor is at least an 8 on a scale of 0-10, with 0 being no benefit or negative effects and 8 or higher meaning I'll get a better outcome by seeking a doctor's help.

Or you can make one factor have special priority, as in this case:

Always give me a 'no' answer to the question "Should I see a doctor about this" if doing so will:

- *Not give me a positive outcome*
- *Cause negative side effects that are worse than the condition*
- *Cost much more than my budget*
- *Take longer and be less effective than doing treatments using a method I know*

You can list one or more conditions that you want to always give you a 'no' answer, if any one of them is enough to make you not want to go to a doctor. Remember, this is personal and unique. It's easier to ask for a 'no' answer when you have specific factors you don't want to compromise on, than to go for the overall rating of seeing a doctor. It's up to you which way to do it.

Always seek a second or third opinion whenever you have an important decision to make, and when in doubt, get professional assistance. Do not use this technique on life or death issues until you feel competent and accurate, and even then, get a second or third opinion. Never let ego put you in danger.

Programming is a method you can use with any dowsing situation that involves a complex question you want to be prepared to use in emergencies at the drop of a hat, or one that you intend to use often. An example would be a water dowser using a brief question like "Where's the best well site?" after programming a very long and detailed question with all the variables he wants to have met. It is good to revisit your original list and programming from time to time to allow you to grow and change factors to suit your needs.

∽

General Checkup List

It's wise to check yourself regularly, not just when you have a symptom you are concerned about. Achieving and maintaining good health is most easily done if you work on prevention. This protocol will give you a snapshot of how you are doing on major subjects that can cause symptoms, but it can also be used as a tool to pinpoint the general cause of a particular symptom. You may find it useful to journal or chart the results of your dowsing so you can see changes over time.

You will be dowsing using a 0 to 10 scale. For us, anything under a 1 is ideal for these factors. Anything over 3 probably is giving you some symptoms, and anything 8 or higher needs immediate attention. It is very important to be detached, not fearful when dowsing these subjects. If you get really low numbers on everything, yet you have health problems, your dowsing is probably inaccurate.

You will be dowsing what level you have of the following subjects:

- Toxicity (energetic or physical)
- Infection (energetic or physical)
- Inflammation
- Trauma
- Parasites (energetic or physical)
- Allergies or sensitivities
- Cancer energy
- Hormonal imbalance/dysfunction

Let's define terms a bit, so that you can understand what you are asking about.

Toxicity

Toxicity is basically anything that your body treats as a poison and has to detoxify. Toxins are not limited to what we think of as poisons; they include just about anything that your body doesn't need and therefore must break down and eliminate. Pesticides and chemicals in your food and water are toxins. But you can also have toxic thoughts, that is, thoughts that create negative energy in you that leads to an imbalance. Even unneeded supplements can be treated as toxins, because they have to be broken down and processed.

Your liver is your detoxifying organ, and if it is not functioning well, you can have a buildup of toxins. If you get a high number for toxicity, determine if it is physical, energetic or both, and how intense each type is, and then check the functioning of your liver on a 0 to 10 scale. It would be excellent if the function of your liver is 8 or higher. Anything less indicates impaired or reduced function.

Reducing toxins you are exposed to at work, home and in your food and thoughts is a great way to help your liver and lower toxicity. Supporting your liver is also helpful, especially as you get older or if you have been exposed to toxins in your job, for example, if you are a hair stylist or a house painter or work in a chemical lab or with pesticides.

(See the sample dowsing question at the end of this section, to be used for all the topics in the list.)

Infection

You can have either a physical or energetic infection. Physical infections are caused by bacteria, viruses and fungi that are either foreign to your body or have become out of balance, mutated or misplaced from their proper location. Energetic infections also can occur in the aura and require treatment.

Natural treatments are available for various types of physical infections, including colloidal silver and some herbs. Drugs are also available for fighting infection, but most of them have side effects that you would be wise to test before using them. Never take any antibiotic unless you have been tested and shown to have a bacterial infection, as antibiotics are only for bacteria, and if you don't have a bacterial infection, taking an antibiotic sets you up later for poor results if you ever need to use one. After using a prescription antibiotic, you would be wise to repopulate your gut microbiome by taking a good probiotic or eating fermented foods.

Inflammation

Due to terrible eating patterns, inflammation is common. A high level of inflammation will give you not only symptoms, but contributes to degenerative disorders. Pain is a common symptom of inflammation. Inflammation can be controlled by diet in many cases, and it is vital to address chronic inflammation, as it is the underlying cause of many diseases, like diabetes, heart disease and Alzheimer's.

If you study and improve your diet, you can reduce inflammation. Inflammation also relates energetically to feeling angry, irritated or under siege. Pay attention to your thoughts, beliefs and your life situation if you have elevated inflammation and try to restore harmony on all levels.

Trauma

Trauma relates to physical damage to some part of the body, as happens in accidents, or emotional trauma, such as a divorce or death in the family. You can have recent trauma causing you a symptom, as in you hit your head on an open cabinet door, and now you have a headache. You can also experience symptoms due to past trauma. Sometimes, scars can contribute to blocked energy flow in your body. If old or new trauma is causing you issues, this number will be above a 1.

Parasites

You can have physical parasites, like tapeworm, or you can have energetic parasites that suck energy from you. There are natural remedies to treat physical parasites, and you can usually get rid of energetic ones by a simple statement of intention.

Allergies & Sensitivities

Allergies and sensitivities are different things that have similar symptoms, so we lump them together. For your purposes, it doesn't matter which you are dealing with. Allergies can be due to something you inhale, something you ingest or something you come into contact with. There are potential allergens all around you, but if you are healthy, they don't spark a reaction. If you have an allergy or an allergic personality, there are a couple possible root causes you should look at:

- Check the function of your liver. If it is overloaded, it can't process histamines, and you will become more sensitive and allergic.
- Check to see if you have leaky gut. Research on the internet if you are not familiar with this term. A leaky gut can lead to allergic food reactions.
- If you have been programmed to believe that life on earth is dangerous or you don't like being here, allergies are one way you may express such an outlook. Changing your beliefs and attitudes will help reduce allergies.

- Avoid anything that can challenge your immune system, like heavy metal exposure and vaccinations, unless you are convinced after researching that they are truly beneficial and necessary.
- Allergies can be due to an event in a past life that led to your death or that of a loved one
- Allergies sometimes energetically are an expression of a strong emotion like grief, rage and anger

Allergic symptoms show up when you get a histamine reaction. They vary greatly depending on the allergen and how you were exposed to it. Anything from a rash to digestive upset or breathing difficulties can be due to an allergic reaction.

Histamine has many functions, including little-known ones like water allocation when you are dehydrated. The best known function has to do with attacking foreign bodies (or anything that appears to be foreign) for disposal. Histamine creates inflammation locally, but that is actually a good thing. It's only when it gets out of hand that you have problems. It is possible to become histamine sensitive, which complicates things further.

Cancer Energy

Please note that we use the phrase 'cancer energy' rather than just asking about cancer. We want to identify the energy of cancer so that it may be transformed before it becomes a physical cancer. You can pick up cancer energy from people and pets who have cancer. I used to pick up cancer energy talking to my mother on the phone after she was diagnosed with lung cancer. When I hung up, I checked and found I often had a 3 on a scale of 10. I cleared it and it went down to 0. But I had to do it often during her last months with the disease, as I have a tendency to take stuff on.

You can also get cancer energy from various imbalances and toxicities, but if it is 3 or under, usually you do not have any physical cancer, and a statement of intention to transform the energy will remove it. If you have a number higher than a 3 or clearing does not change the number at all, then you need to do more specific dowsing. If the number is 8 or higher, get a second opinion or see your doctor.

There are many holistic methods for treating cancer, and you can use dowsing to choose one that will help you reach your goals. If you go the conventional route, your options are limited, and you need to know in advance that radiation and chemotherapy have very strong negative side effects for most people. Get a second and a third opinion before choosing what to do, and make sure your dowsing and intuition agree with whatever option you choose. There is no one right way for everyone, and don't be pressured into doing what everyone else does unless you feel confident it is best for you.

The most important thing is not to let fear take over if you dowse that you have significant cancer energy. Maybe your dowsing is wrong. Get a second opinion. If your dowsing is correct, you have taken a step towards health by discovering this situation. You are already way better off than if you didn't know. In many cases, an early warning translates into a cure.

Hormonal Imbalance/Dysfunction

A hormone is a substance your body produces that is a sort of messenger that causes an effect or physiological action. You have hormones that control all aspects of life, though they are still barely understood. Leptin is a hormone that deals with appetite; melatonin helps you sleep; sex hormones allow you to reproduce; insulin helps you digest food; cortisol helps you deal with stress, and so on.

When hormones are imbalanced, the physiological activity they control gets out of whack. Hormone imbalance and dysfunction is a very complicated subject that usually requires professional consultation to resolve, because the hormones don't act totally independent of one another, and the more imbalance you have, often, the more hormones and systems are affected.

Circadian rhythms and nutrition have a powerful effect on hormone balance and function, so they are two topics to research if you get a 3 or higher for this subject on a scale of 10. It is possible if you improve your diet and circadian cycles, you will rebalance your hormones. It can take time to rebalance hormones, so be patient, but do consult a professional if you have concerns about your health.

The dowsing question we use for all of the above topics is:

On a scale of 0 to 10, with 0 being none and 10 being the most I can have, what level of _____ (insert one of the terms from the above list) is present in any level of my body at this time?

The best answer to get for this question is 0 to 1. For us, once the number reaches 3, there are probably symptoms, and 8 or higher means you need to take action soon to restore balance and health.

∾

Checking Organs & Systems

YOUR PHYSICAL BODY has organs that have specific functions. For example, your liver detoxifies your system. In reality, your organs often have multiple functions, and each organ is part of a bigger system. The digestive system includes a number of organs. Some organs are part of more than one system, so you will see overlap and synergy. Try to remember that modern science still only knows a tiny bit of what is really going on in the body, and even in the last 25 years, our understanding of how the body works has changed dramatically. The human body is a very complex structure, so this is of necessity a very abbreviated version of what we now know. You may look these up online to get more complete definitions.

You can check the function of your major organs or systems using a 0-10 scale, where 8 or higher indicates a good to excellent level of functioning. Your question will be very important, because it will affect your answer.

Is your intention to compare the function of your organ with that of a person of your age and gender in your country? Or do you just want an overall level of function that is not so specific, that averages across age and gender and culture? You could get two totally different answers depending on how you word your question and define terms.

As we age, our body sometimes loses function. You theoretically might not even be able to have the level of function at 65 that someone has at 25, depending on what you are talking about. And men and women often seen different results in terms of function.

But then, what if you want to be a 'young' 65? Why settle for reduced function if you don't need to? Your question therefore will reflect your own goals and your perspective on age and health. If you buy into the common modern belief that as you age, you fall apart, you will be coming from a different direction entirely than someone who believes age is just a number and intends to be vital and active until the day they die.

We are pointing this out simply so that you can understand that your answer may vary a lot depending on your attitudes, beliefs and point of view, in addition to the wording of your question. You can convince yourself of this by asking different versions of the same questions.

Here's a question that uses the +10 to -10 scale and has 0 as average for your age, gender and culture:

On a scale of +10 to -10, with 0 being average for my gender, age and culture, what is the overall physical health of my _____ System (example: circulatory) at this time?

An answer of 0 means you are average for the group you are comparing yourself to. A positive number means better than average, while a negative number means below average. If you are comparing yourself to Americans of your age, you probably should not settle for an answer of 0, because the average American is not very healthy. (See how defining terms makes a difference in the answer?)

Or you can use a 0-10 scale that gives you an estimate of your function based on what is theoretically optimal for your body at this time:

On a scale of 0 to 10, with 10 being the best possible function for my body at this time, what is the overall physical health of my _____System (or name an organ) at this time?

You can substitute an organ instead of a system in the above questions. We regard 8 or above as good to excellent for this question.

What if your numbers dismay you? Take a deep breath and be grateful that you have dowsing to give you early warning. Secondly, if the numbers look really bad, get a second or third opinion. Dowsing is not 100%, and you may not be dowsing accurately. Instead, you may be dowsing what you fear is true, which isn't really dowsing; it's allowing your emotions to hijack the process.

Bottom line, knowledge is power. If you intuitively sense that the low number is correct, then use dowsing to determine the best way to remedy the situation. Be in this for the long haul. You can't get instant health, and it will require some kind of investment and commitment on your part, but isn't it worth it to feel good and have energy and live the way you want?

Here is a brief list of systems for testing with very abbreviated summaries of function:

Nervous System: Receives incoming information (senses). Sends messages to the body about how to react. Includes: central nervous system (brain) and peripheral nerves.

Circulatory System: Transports oxygen, waste, nutrients, hormones, heat, etc... around the body and consists of heart, arteries, veins.

Reproductive System: Produces sex cells (sperm and eggs). Produces sex hormones (testosterone, estrogen). Nurtures the unborn baby (fetus). Includes ovaries, uterus, testes.

Endocrine System: Controls body functions using chemicals messengers called hormones. Consists of glands like thyroid, adrenals, pancreas.

Digestive System: Breaks down food into smaller molecules. Absorbs these nutrients into the body. Includes stomach, intestines, mouth, throat, liver, pancreas, gall bladder.

Urinary System: Cleanses the blood. Rids the body of wastes. Maintains salt and water balance. Includes kidneys and bladder.

Skeletal System: Provides shape and structure to the body. Allows for movement. Protects vital organs. Produces blood cells. Includes bones, ligaments, tendons, cartilage.

Respiratory System: Brings oxygen to the body, gets rid of carbon dioxide. Includes the lungs.

Muscle System: Allows for movement of the body. Keeps head in position. Provides heat. Consists of muscles, sometimes includes the heart.

Integumentary System: Protects the body from invaders by providing a tough protective layer. Warms the body. Cools the body. Includes hair, skin, nails.

Lymphatic System: Maintains fluid balance and fights infections, including almost 600 nodes and a vast network that penetrates most tissues.

Immune System: Fights disease. Composed of specialized white blood cells. Works in concert with the lymphatic system.

Allow yourself to get whatever the accurate answer is. By knowing in advance that you have reduced or impaired function in one or more systems, that provides you with the basis for working to harmonize and restore them to excellent function. As with lab tests, your dowsing answer is just a snapshot of what is going on at this time. It is NOT an indication of a permanent condition. Look at your answers as starting points for building the health you want. Also, be aware that function changes with time due to changing stress and pressures. So check in periodically to see how things are going.

∼

Everyday Health: Diet, Supplements, Sleep & Exercise

THIS IS GOING to be perhaps the biggest section in the book, as it covers what is most important: your everyday choices that either build or destroy health.

While it is a mistake to think that food and exercise are the only factors in our health and fitness, they are important in terms of creating or destroying health, and dowsing about them will help you customize your diet and also permit you to improve and change it as you evolve. A good plan in general is to have a nutrient-dense eating program and plenty of pure water, to modify it over time as you observe effects, to choose supplements to shore up weak points in your plan and to have an exercise regimen that helps you achieve your fitness goals. We will also present some little-known, surprising factors that can affect your success.

Our approach illustrates our personal viewpoint that health is under your control, that instant health is not a realistic goal and that it takes commitment and an investment on your part to create good health. If you are patient and committed, you can use health dowsing to help you create the level of health you desire, whether it's just to get rid of migraines or joint pain, or you want to be fit enough to easily run a marathon. If on the other hand, you believe you are a prisoner of your genetics, that restricted outlook will limit your success, so examine your overall belief in how much you are in control of your health, because that is a key factor in your success or failure to attain your health goals.

Water

Before humans became 'civilized' and began living in large groups, they drank mostly water. Their water came from streams and glacial meltwater and was pure and in many cases infused with health-giving minerals. In more modern times, humans created beverages that came in handy as a substitute for water when clean water wasn't available or safe to drink, as in most early cities and villages, or for spiritual and later, entertainment purposes, as in alcoholic beverages.

In recent times, carbonated and alcoholic beverages and bottled water have become commonplace, and coffee seems to be the drink of choice in hectic modern society. Beverages that once were only consumed rarely, if at all, have become easily obtainable in many cultures.

This change has not contributed to the health of humans, because the ingredients of those drinks are not healthy when ingested frequently or in quantity. Water is still the best beverage you can drink, as it is required for many physiological processes. Most of your body is composed of water, and soda, beer and coffee have a dehydrating effect instead of a hydrating one. If you drink caffeinated or alcoholic beverages, it's like drinking negative water. In addition, the caffeine, sugar, artificial chemicals and acids have a detrimental effect on many of your organs and their function. But even if you know this, and you are committed to drinking more water, how pure is your water?

Tap water is not pure. A quick bit of research reveals levels of lead, nitrates, arsenic and other pollutants are often present, as well as there being a 1 in 4 chance (if you live in the US) that your city water is unsafe to drink or is not properly monitored for contaminants. Chlorine and fluoride are bad for your gut and skin microbiota (the tiny organisms that keep those areas healthy). If you use tap water, you need to filter it, both for drinking and for washing. There are many methods of filtration that range from cheap to very expensive. You can't always go by price to get the best one for your water and your needs, though.

There is no substitute for research and due diligence. This is an example of where it is simply lazy to use dowsing instead of researching a topic. Your brain is powerful. Use it. Get online and read about water purity and filtration. Your intuition will begin to lean in a certain direction.

Once you have done all you can to use the rational mind, if you aren't 100% sure that one option is best, then it's time to dowse which of the options are best for your needs. Dowsing is for getting answer to questions your rational mind cannot answer. Here's a sample question:

On a scale of +10 to -10, with 0 being neutral and positive numbers meaning purer and healthier for my physical needs, what is the level in effects of using _____(name the method) to filter my _____(name the water source, as in tap water or well water or bottled water)?

A number of +8 or higher is what we use as the cutoff for investing in anything. You want significant positive change, not just slight improvement. It is possible you can get a 0 or even a negative number if the method would be worse than what you now do or would contaminate the water or make it less healthy, or if it just isn't worth the money it costs.

Another use of dowsing with respect to water concerns altering the energy of water, as was demonstrated by Dr. Emoto. Water has the ability to carry energies, which means you can imprint it using intention or by anchoring your intention with something like a customized symbol. This process comes in handy in situations like this:

- You have good well water, but want to enhance it for a certain goal
- You are being forced to drink water of questionable energy, and you want to improve it
- You just want to show gratitude to Nature for providing you with life-giving resources like pure water

A simple statement of intention, or one anchored by something like a crystal or symbol, is useful in these situations. Remember, dowsing doesn't change energies, but you can use dowsing to reveal what method will be most effective for your particular goals.

An example is you want to help your dog be healthy or recover from surgery, so you dowse the following:

What is the overall level in effects on the long term health of my dog on a 0-10 scale, with 8 or higher being significantly better, if I use a symbol to energize his water for healing by putting it on a card under his bowl?

If you get less than 8, don't bother. If you get 8 or more, then ask this:

What is the long term level in effects using the same scale of using a customized symbol? Of using a symbol known to me?

Go with the one that gives the best number, if it is 8 or higher, and then you have to dowse to figure out what the symbol is. A known symbol may be a cross or an ohm or a star of David, anything that is meaningful to you. A customized symbol means you make the symbol yourself, either using your intuition or dowsing it stroke for stroke as you draw it. When you think you have the right symbol, dowse again what the effect of using it will be, just to make sure.

Food

Don't diet. Instead, eat good food. As you get a healthier eating plan and lifestyle, any extra weight you have can come off. It may take a number of years and layers of changes, because excess weight is a hugely complex topic, but all that matters is that you intend to create good health. Our point is this: excess weight is not solely about calories taken in and calories burned, which explains the failure of most dietary plans. We discuss some other factors at the end of this chapter. If you have excess weight, you would be wise to address those rather than jump on a fad diet.

There is no one perfect eating plan, no matter what anyone tells you. That is because frankly, we don't know nearly enough about human biology to make that kind of claim. However, it does seem logical that we are in general more likely to be healthy if we eat the way we are biologically designed to eat.

Even that simple statement is fraught with complexities. We can extrapolate some facts by looking at dentition (our teeth), the length of our gut, our digestive enzymes and things like that. Those facts point to humans as being omnivorous. That means, we can eat anything. We are not designed to be exclusively vegetarians. Our guts are nowhere near as long or complex as those of horses, cattle and other vegetarian animals. We don't have the gut flora to deal with cellulose and break down plant cells, we don't have multiple stomachs and we don't have the ever-growing teeth for grinding down plant material. We do better on a mixture of foods. Another issue is that herbivores are designed to be able to extract nutrition, such as minerals, from plant material, but humans are far less able to utilize inorganic minerals.

Yet we are not obligate carnivores like cats. We cannot stay well by eating mostly animal protein. Obligate carnivores have short guts and teeth and enzymes for breaking down animal material. Humans are in between carnivores and herbivores in terms of design.

Livestock seem to be able to subsist on diets high in grains, but in nature, they don't eat grain. Probably the reason we don't notice this is that livestock are fattened for slaughter at a fairly young age, so long-term health issues don't matter, and grain is good at fattening animals. You might ask why, then, are grains (fruits from cereal grasses) such a big part of human diet for thousands of years, if grains are not a natural food for us? While seeds and nuts can be a good source of protein, plants have evolved many chemical protections to prevent animals from eating their reproductive parts. Allergies, inflammation and digestive problems can occur if you eat large quantities of seeds and nuts or if your digestion is less than optimal. (In fact, if you grain a horse regularly, it often develops ulcers, which lead to all kinds of health issues).

The plants don't want you to eat their seeds and fruits (which are their way to reproduce), so they make it hard to gather them and to extract nutrition from them and in extreme cases, even have them poison you. Yes, that is why some fruits and seeds are poisonous, to keep them from being eaten. (Other plants have taken the exact opposite approach and have made it possible to grow a new plant only after the seed passes through the digestive tract of an animal, but this is more rare, as it ties reproductive success to another species.)

Processed grains that become bleached flour with all the nutrients removed and then get baked into bread lack most of the value the original grains had, but sometimes still have irritating substances. This is a second reason not to make grains a big part of your diet, because you won't get anything but empty calories, and you will start seeing inflammation and insulin and leptin resistance, which leads to all kinds of diseases. If you have cravings and are always hungry, it is a sign of an imbalance. Your body knows whether it is being fed good food. You will stay hungry until you deliver what it needs, and what it needs is vitamins, minerals, enzymes and other nutrition.

Natural humans ate what was available in quantities proportional to how much effort it was to obtain the foods. The harder and more dangerous, the less often it was eaten. (This is one reason we aren't designed to ingest a lot of alcohol. It used to be very rare.) They would binge on whatever was in season, then not get any of that fruit or vegetable until the next season. These days, we have no regard for what is in season, which is a shame, because our bodies are calibrated to note the composition of nutrients in our diet in order to respond to the season.

Supplements

Ideally, if your diet is 'good,' you should not need supplements. The sad fact is that most modern diets are very deficient due to factory farming, pesticide use and mineral-depleted soils. If you are not a knowledgeable organic gardener growing your own food, you are probably not getting the nutrition you need from your diet. Supplements are the answer to that issue.

Supplements have long been dissed by conventional medicine. Doctors say you just pee away the vitamins. And this is in fact true if you buy cheap vitamins that are not bioavailable. If your body cannot utilize a nutrient in the form presented to it, it is not bioavailable. An example is oyster shell calcium. The human body is not adept at absorbing and using inorganic minerals, like the calcium from oyster shells.

It is also true if you have leaky gut, which is an undiagnosed epidemic in this society. Leaky gut makes you unable to extract nutrition from what you eat and leads to allergies and autoimmune reactions. Also, if your gut microbiome is damaged or imbalanced, you won't get proper nutrients from your food.

Don't spend money on supplements until you heal your digestion and are convinced you are absorbing your nutrients, and if you buy vitamins and minerals, make sure they are bioavailable. Horses and cows can extract some nutrition from inorganic minerals, but humans don't have nearly the ability that herbivores have. When you dowse supplements, bioavailability for your system is vital.

Dowsing is a good way to choose supplements for your goals. You can go for overall good health (however you define that), or you can focus on healing a single condition or deficiency. We recommend that you do NOT supplement a single mineral or vitamin unless you have proof that you have a deficiency in that item, and even then, be very cautious, because most minerals and vitamins work in concert with others, and by adding a lot of one, you will imbalance the other(s).

Here is an example. It is a pretty good bet that most people are deficient in the fat-soluble vitamins A, K (especially K2) and D. These vitamins are obtained from foods that are no longer eaten by most folks, like organ meats, fish oils and eggs and dairy products from pastured animals. Deficiencies in these vitamins are insidious and take years to allow disease to develop. Loading just one of these vitamins or taking them in improper proportions will not help you, and may do more harm than good.

The same is true for zinc (Zn) and copper (Cu). Also for calcium (Ca) and magnesium (Mg), which work in concert. In the case of the latter, most people are magnesium deficient, yet doctors are now telling people to load calcium, which for a lot of reasons (including if you are K2 deficient, which most people are, the Ca won't end up in the right place), only makes things worse. Studying up on the basics of these elements will help you, as will consulting a good holistic professional. Don't rely solely on dowsing if you have a very limited understanding of how vitamins and minerals work (and this is true for most people, including allopathic doctors).

Dowsing supplements requires an excellent question. You can't use vague terms like 'good'; you need to have a very specific and detailed goal. Take time to work these things out before formulating your dowsing question. Use scales so that you can see different shades of quality and efficacy among supplements.

There are many ways of asking the question. This is one that might be useful if you are standing in the health food store looking at shelves of the same vitamin or remedy:

Will supplementation by any of these products be an 8 or higher on a scale of 10 (with 10 being the most helpful) for creating excellent immune balance/good energy levels/excellent physical function for my body (fill in whatever your goal is) for me at this time when taken as directed for at least 90 days?

Notice you need to include dosage, timing ('at this time') and your goal if you want an accurate answer. There are many ways you can modify this question. Just make sure it contains every element that matters to you and that can affect results. And also include the understanding that it must be bioavailable for your system at this time. If you can't find any that test well, it might be that you have digestive issues that you need to address first.

After you choose a supplement, you also need to test it to see if adding it to your regular program (assuming you take other supplements) is a good idea. Sometimes the interaction of things lessens efficacy.

Here is a question you can use which assumes you already have dowsed your overall program (the overall program should be at least an 8 for your goals), and the supplement itself is at least an 8 for your needs:

What is the overall effectiveness of my entire program of supplements for my health goals on a scale of 0 to 10 at this time if I include this new product at the recommended dosage?

If you get less than an 8, adding the product is not a good idea. Don't weaken your program by taking too many things at once, and avoid negative interactions.

Another thing to dowse is the level of side effects if you take the product that dowsed as best for you. You can include that in your question and ask that only products with side effects that are low (like 'less than 1 on a scale of 0-10') be given a number of 8 or higher. Or you can test side effects after you dowse the best product for your goals. Detoxes and allergic reactions can be winnowed out or dealt with if you dowse side effects. There are details on this process in a later section of this chapter.

Sensitive people will find they may be unable to deal with binders and fillers in some supplements. It isn't the supplement itself that is bothering you, it's the inactive ingredients. This is especially true for some broad spectrum vitamins. Titanium dioxide is an example of a supposedly inert ingredient that may bother you. You can include these concerns in your question, having it understood that you want to get a low number if any of the above are true.

We recommend that you dowse your program and supplements together and individually every month, as you are changing. Most supplements are meant for temporary or intermittent use, and once you no longer need them, you can and should eliminate them to prevent taxing your liver.

Some vitamins that you probably will need to take regularly or intermittently include a broad spectrum of B vitamins, Vitamin C, a good K2/A/D combination and Mg. You can go online and look up symptoms of deficiency for these vitamins to see if you fit the profile, but more than likely, you are low on K2/A/D at the very least, and most people benefit from high quality B complex, C and Mg supplements on occasion. For the K2/A/D supplementation, we prefer a food-type supplement as recommended by the Weston A. Price Foundation, that is a proven combination of cod liver oil and butter oil. See the Resources for a link.

Exercise Regimens

Fitness, strength and flexibility improve the quality of life. Your body is intended for movement. If modern life has you sitting for hours every day, that is not going to contribute to health and fitness.

Walking is the best exercise you can do. People are designed to walk. It doesn't cost money to walk, and almost anyone can do it. Even if you are not healthy, you can usually get started on a walking program and just increase the distance with time.

Parking far from where you are going or taking the stairs instead of the elevators can be a big help. Walk instead of driving. Don't use the excuse of not having time. Make the time.

If all you do is walk a good distance regularly, you will improve your health. When you feel you are ready for a more challenging exercise program, there are many types from which to choose, like cardiovascular exercise, weight lifting, yoga and tai chi. It is wise to check with your doctor before embarking on a fitness regime if you have any physical issues.

There are benefits to all kinds of exercise, but you are unique, and what works for someone else may not be as beneficial for you. It might even be detrimental to your health. If you are the slightest bit tuned in to your intuition, you will find yourself drawn to a particular program. Listen to your Inner Voice. Then, if you have any doubts about committing, use dowsing to discover how useful it will be for you. Don't make the mistake of thinking that yoga and tai chi are for sissies; they are just a gentler way of strengthening you.

As you travel the path to fitness, you may find you want to make changes to your program. Be open to that and use dowsing to help you choose well.

Your dowsing, as always, starts with your having clear goals before you ask your question. Are you preparing for a marathon and desire to run competitively, or do you merely want to see significant improvement in your strength or endurance? Your goals are unique to you and will affect the answer you get. Money and time can also be a factor you want to include. If you are looking for ways to become fit that take the least time, the least money and offer the most benefit, include those factors. If money and time are no object, fine. Under no circumstances should you do exercise you don't enjoy, so be sure to include enjoyment as a factor in your question.

Here's a sample question you might use when you are ranking fitness programs:

On a scale of +10 to -10, with 0 being no benefit, negative numbers being detrimental and positive numbers being beneficial for reaching my goals, what is the overall level in effects for my fitness goals of my taking the beginner's tai chi class at the Y?

This question assumes you have already dowsed that tai chi as a method is highly beneficial for you, and you are trying to find the best way to learn. You could also test a particular DVD training.

Dowsing is a way of taking a bunch of options and slowly paring them down until you come up with one method that offers the most benefit to you. This process is the same in general for most health questions.

Step 1: write down your goals and be very complete and specific

Step 2: form a very detailed dowsing question using an appropriate scale

Step 3: dowse a list of options, and discard any that come up less than 8

Step 4: review your question and make it more detailed if you have too many options left and re-dowse the remaining options to narrow the field

Step 5: when you have one option left, you are ready to take action

What if you don't get any that are 8 or higher? Don't invest in something that doesn't test well. Go back to your goals and revise them, because it may be that your intuition is not giving you answers so that you can revise your goals.

If you find yourself not following through on your program or it gets stale, dowse again and see if it's time for a change.

Sleep

There is a reason that sleep deprivation is used as a form of torture and to break people down. Your body requires sleep to repair. You cannot live well on short sleep for very long. There is no substitute for having that down time and letting your body rebuild and repair.

Modern humans mistakenly think that caffeine and sugar are a substitute for a good night's sleep. They think if they can show up at work and appear alert and do their job, they are OK. They are wrong. If you care about your health, make an effort to get good sleep and plenty of it each night. Do not indulge in the common behaviors that erode health. Not only is lack of sleep unhealthy, using caffeine, sugar or drugs to avoid sleeping or compensate for poor sleep puts a load on your adrenals and liver and can lead to dis-ease. Using drugs to help you sleep comes with side effects, so definitely avoid that, or if you must, only do it rarely.

You are unique in terms of how much sleep you need in order to be healthy, but most people do best on 8 hours a night. In order to sleep well, don't eat or drink after sunset or 6 or 7pm, and eliminate all sources of EMF (electromagnetic frequencies) in your bedroom. No phones, no chargers, no TVs, not even a clock radio. Remove all manmade light as well.

There isn't a lot to dowse about regarding sleep unless you find yourself unable to fall asleep or stay asleep. If you have adopted the above suggestions and you still cannot sleep well, there are many possible factors, because sleep is very complex. The first place to start is to rectify your circadian rhythms. Even if they are not the only problem you have, fixing them is vital to your health. The next section will give you some suggestions and background. Another major issue with modern humans is stress. Reduce stress in order to get a good night's sleep.

If you want to dowse what effect something is having on your getting a good, restful and restorative night's sleep, here is a sample question:

On a +10 to -10 scale, with 0 being no effect, what is the overall level in effects on my getting a good night's sleep of _____(eating____, drinking_____, doing this_____) at the frequency I am now doing it?

Be sure you previously defined what a good night's sleep is to you. There are a number of factors. It isn't just getting 8 hours. It could include sleeping through the night, getting restorative sleep (as in getting enough REM sleep), and waking up feeling refreshed and rested. It might even include not having frequent nightmares or sweats. Write down everything in your journal so you can go back and evaluate your success.

Factors You May Not Know About

Circadian rhythms are biological patterns that are tuned to a 24-hour clock. They have been shown to be present in most life forms on earth, for obvious reasons. As with a lot about health, science still doesn't know the whole story on circadian rhythms, and as research continues, it appears they affect a lot of things beyond sleep.

At this point, the most important fact we can share with you is that your circadian rhythms are set by sunlight. This becomes a problem for modern humans who spend so little time outside in natural light. Natural light has way more effects than just helping you form vitamin D. Ancient cultures knew the value of the sun. The sun salutation in yoga and facing east to pray or orienting your home to face east are manifestations of the awareness of the importance of the sun in our lives.

Spend as much time as you can outdoors in the sun. If you live at a far north or far south latitude, it will be hard for you to get enough sunshine. Do your best.

When you are out in the sun, your eyes are absorbing the EMFs from the sun and your body is being attuned to various functions and cycles by that light that lands on your eyes. Wearing sunglasses can prevent you from using the sun's rays properly.

Your skin has a complex microbiome and responds to sunlight. Using a chemically-laden sunscreen not only is harmful to your skin microorganisms, but also defeats the sun's function. If you are not convinced of the dangers of these modern habits, do some research online.

In addition to being out in sunlight and seeing it and not blocking it on your skin (within reason), there is another, more insidious modern problem you need to address. Sunlight is natural. But in the past 100+ years, manmade EMFs have proliferated and changed our lifestyle, overpowering natural light or even replacing it. Not only are there manmade lights to fool your body into thinking it's daytime when it's night, computers, phones, TVs and tablets have screens that emit an unnatural, abnormally unbalanced stream of 'blue' light that fools your eyes into thinking it is daytime at all times of day, because the composition of the light those things emit is like morning light. Not only does this mess up your circadian rhythms, it has a negative effect on your eyes and your eyesight. Blueblocker glasses are becoming popular, and we advise you to research them and get a good pair and wear them. But don't look at screens after sunset, no matter what.

Your body needs to know it's nighttime to prepare you to fall asleep. We saw a dramatic change in our ability to get drowsy when we stopped using electric light after dark. We use oil lanterns which don't emit unnatural light. The natural darkness instructs your body to make melatonin, which helps you sleep. It's more complex than that, but the bottom line is natural is good for you. Unnatural EMFs have lots of negative effects. Blue light creates eye problems and messes up your sleep, but those are just the proximate effects. It may well be that obesity and degenerative diseases like diabetes are on the rise due to spending so much time staring at screens. If you don't believe us, do some research online and read some books on this subject.

We accept so much as 'natural' that isn't, simply because we grew up with those things. We have been programmed to think they are conveniences, and some of them are, but in all cases, the programming was done mainly to sell things to us, not to make our lives better.

An example is that smart phones and cell phones didn't exist when we were children, and guess what, we managed without them. When I think about washing dishes by hand vs. using a dishwasher (and this comparison goes for almost all household appliances), the amount of effort expended on the overall job is pretty much equal whether I use a modern appliance or do the dishes by hand. When our dishwasher was broken, we did all the dishes by hand. It wasn't much different in terms of time and effort, and frankly, it used less electricity.

Our Roomba seemed indispensable with our 12 pets shedding hair and dragging dirt into the house through the pet door, but after a while, I noticed that taking a mop and just sweeping once a day seemed to be about as effective, and although it took me a few minutes, it cost no electricity or big cash outlay to buy the appliance.

The promises of modern conveniences hinted at greater freedom in return for the cost, but we seem to have swapped time for electric bills and expensive gadgets, and it isn't immediately obvious to me how liberating that is. In fact, I think it's just the opposite. The more bills you have to pay, the more money you need, and the more enslaved you are to a job you might hate. Convincing you that you need to buy things is a great way to rob you of freedom of choice.

Some modern conveniences have become necessities—certainly in some locations, you need a car, for example, but for your health, it is wise to limit, offset and eliminate devices, habits and thought patterns that take a toll on your health.

The final point we want to share is that the totality of what Science claims to know about health at this time is such a small percent of all the things that relate to health that it is wise to keep a very open mind and not regard what Science currently says as the whole truth, because it is a very incomplete truth. Think about how two hundred years ago, people were bled by doctors to heal them. Doctors didn't wash their hands before or after surgery. Opium was put in over-the-counter medications and prescribed for children. Yet in those days, they thought they were advanced.

What we do now will be looked on two hundred years from now in some cases as horrific. (Vaccinations come to mind). It's hard to see it when you've been programmed to accept modern health care as perfect and advanced, but we really don't know it all; no one does. Dowsing will help you find the best path for your goals, but you need to keep an open mind.

∼

Allergies & Sensitivities

Liver Overload Is A Symptom & Contributing Factor

Allergies and sensitivities of all kinds are becoming more common. This has to do with modern life. There are far more toxins in the environment than there were two or three generations ago, toxins in air, water and food that lead to leaky gut and immune issues.

The liver is tasked with breaking down histamine, which is the substance your body secretes when there is inflammation or it senses attack by a foreign body. Histamine has other roles as well, and you would be well-advised to study up online about them if you have a tendency to allergies. For example, histamine is a sort of referee when you become dehydrated, as it decides what gets priority for the little water that is available. This might hint that being dehydrated exacerbates the situation by getting histamine active, so be sure to stay fully hydrated if you have an allergic personality.

Back to the liver, if it is overloaded doing its job breaking down toxins and disassembling and recycling compounds like histamine, you can end up with too much histamine or too many toxins. Anyone who has lots of allergies should dowse the level of function of their liver and then dowse for remedies if the function is below 8 on a scale of 10. Here are some questions to use:

On a scale of 0 to 10, with 8 or higher being good or better, what is the overall function of my liver at this time?

Anything below an 8 would benefit from help of some kind.

On a scale of 0 to 10, with 8 or better meaning it is a good choice for healing my liver quickly, effectively and affordably, how does _____(name the supplement) rate, taken as directed for at least 30 days?

There are many herbal remedies for liver problems, and we suggest you research online and make a list before dowsing. You can use this same question, substituting the brand name of the supplement that tests best, to choose the exact brand at your health food store. (Always test for side effects, especially if you have an allergic personality.)

Milk thistle in various forms is one of the most popular liver remedies, but over the years, we have found that it does not always test as the best one to take. Dowse a few different ones until you find one that tests 8 or better.

On a scale of 0 to 10, with 3 or more being noticeably negative, what level of side effects overall will I experience if I take _____(name the remedy) as directed for at least 30 days to restore my liver?

We try to avoid using anything that gives a 3 or higher in side effects. If you get too high a number, find a different liver support product. If everything you test gives you a 3 or more, you may need to go back and test lower dosages of the same products, or else dowse about getting the help of a health care professional for your liver issues.

If your liver is testing as low in function, remove as many toxins as possible from your diet and environment. Many people don't understand that anything you put into your body that is not needed and used is regarded and treated as a toxin. This goes for supplements that aren't doing you any good. It loads your liver to take a lot of supplements that aren't really needed. This is yet another reason to test your supplements and your whole supplement program. Obviously, drugs and alcohol need to be eliminated from the diet if you have liver issues. If you are on prescription drugs, you can check online for warnings about liver effects and talk to your doctor about using something less problematic.

Another challenge the liver faces is that it doesn't simply detoxify physical toxins. The liver is the seat of anger and rage in the body, and if you are processing large amounts of anger, it puts a load on your liver. If you live in a toxic environmental energy situation, your liver is being asked to work overtime. When the liver is overloaded by what it is processing, physical or energetic, it loses function. So, if you are in a situation at home or work that triggers a lot of anger, suppressed or not, find a way to deal with the anger instead of burying it. We suggest tapping (EFT) or the Emotion Code. Anger is bad for your health if you hang onto it. If your living or workspace are toxic, do regular space clearings to harmonize the energies.

Histamine Intolerance

Histamine intolerance is becoming recognized as something that can contribute to allergies and other symptoms, though it is not an allergy as such. There are many good references online to this topic, along with lists of symptoms and suggested diets. Check it out and then use dowsing to determine if you have this issue and which dietary suggestions would be best for you. We won't go into a lot of detail on this condition, as it is not an allergy as such, but if you have a lot of allergies, we suggest you research this topic.

Beliefs, Past Lives & Attitudes

Whether conscious or subconscious, the attitude that life on earth is dangerous and that you are powerless to avoid the dangers can lead to the manifestation of allergies. Another root cause is irritation and inflammation of a mental-emotional nature, such as being angry at being here on earth and feeling you lack proper boundaries for protection or believe you are or must be hypersensitive (overly empathetic). Lastly, allergies sometimes are a sign of inner crying by someone who did not get nourished as a child. If you have an allergic personality, you would be wise to check beliefs and attitudes and clear them, as discussed in the 'Subconscious Beliefs' section later in this chapter.

A doctor may tell you that your chances of being allergic are greater if your mother and/or father were allergic. This is not only true because of genetic factors, but epigenetic factors that pass trauma energy down through generations. That trauma energy can manifest as an allergy.

This also happens in past lives, and we have had very good success at clearing allergies by clearing past life trauma that triggered the allergy in this lifetime (if that is the root cause). It does not always succeed, but it has given us remarkable success, and the beauty of it is that there are no negative side effects, it costs nothing except a little time, and it does you good regardless of the results with the allergy. So clearing past lives is the method we will address for remedying allergies in this section.

Discovering Allergies With Dowsing

Warning: Never expose yourself to any substance you have a potential anaphylactic reaction to, as that is life and death, and you must simply eliminate such substances/allergens forever from your diet for safety's sake.

In order to get rid of allergies, you need to first identify them. Dowsing is a good tool, as long as you are a competent dowser.

Allergens, things that stimulate an allergic response, generally come to you in one of three ways: ingestion, breathing or contact. Ingestion is eating or drinking. The air can have all kinds of pollen and other irritants that give you a reaction when you breathe them. And contact allergies often arise from cleaning and personal care products.

If you have food allergies, the elimination diet is a good test. If you take an item out of your diet for two weeks, and then reintroduce it, you will get symptoms if you are allergic to it. This is a good way to ferret out allergens or to confirm the results of your dowsing.

One approach to discovering about allergies is if you have what you think is an allergic reaction, but you aren't sure, dowse using this question:

Is the _____(describe the symptom, like skin rash) I have experienced this past week caused directly or indirectly by an allergic or sensitivity reaction?

If you get a 'no', then you need to explore other possibilities. If you get a 'yes', then ask:

How am I being exposed to this substance? Inhalation? Ingestion? Contact?

You will get a 'yes' for the exposure type. If you get more than one, it could be because you are responding to a combination of allergens, but usually, you will get only one method of exposure. That will help you limit the field of possible allergens.

You can find a list of possible allergens online if you want to do a thorough test. Or you can just check out a few items, such as if you recently changed shampoos or started eating something new. If you have a long list of possible allergens, use list dowsing to identify the culprit. Here is a possible question you can use while saying or pointing to each item:

Please give me a 'yes' response when I say (or point) to the item that is causing my allergic reaction.

If you just want to check a few items you suspect, here is a question to use:

On a 0 to 10 scale, with 0 being no allergy or sensitivity, how allergic or sensitive am I to _____(name the substance) at this time?

A 0 means you are not allergic, and a 1 to 3 response usually means you are mildly sensitive. 8 or higher means you are very sensitive. This question includes the concepts of allergy and sensitivity, as they are medically somewhat different, but they can display the same symptoms.

Usually, you have suspicions about food allergies, because you get symptoms when you eat certain things. Whether it's a rash or indigestion, you want to identify the cause. It is pretty tricky at times, because it can take 48 hours for a symptom to show up. Also, combinations of allergens can boost the reaction to much higher than an individual allergen would cause.

One thing is for sure. The more allergies you have, the closer you need to look at your liver, and if the allergies are food allergies, you need to heal your gut and reduce the inflammatory response. If you have longstanding or many allergies, it is probably wise to work with a holistic practitioner. We say holistic, because only a holistic practitioner will address the root cause and help your body heal and become well. If all you care about is suppressing a symptom, go to a conventional doctor, but be aware that taking drugs of any kind gives you side effects while not healing the root cause of your issue and will almost certainly load your liver further. It's your choice how to deal with allergies, but we prefer to heal them.

Clearing Allergies

In addition to the physical suggestions we or your doctor might make, you can do energy clearing to help remove the cause of the allergic response. This has worked in a significant number of cases for us. It may or may not work for you, but it's relatively easy to do, there are no negative side effects, and it's free, so why not give it a try?

Before I go through the process, here's a client's story. Some years ago, I worked with a client who had an allergy he wanted to be rid of. He described it as an allergy to seafood. He didn't name a particular type of seafood, and he didn't tell me symptoms. He merely said he'd been avoiding seafood, because it gave him a reaction, and he'd like to heal that. So we used the process I am describing in this section. We identified a couple of past lives contributing to a seafood allergy, and we cleared the energies. I then told him what I told all clients, that this didn't mean he was 'cured', but that if he felt good about it, he could try a very small amount of seafood sometime when it didn't matter if he had a reaction, just to test the results of the clearing.

The next time we worked together, he told me incidentally that he was very pleased with the results of his clearing for seafood. He said that he had ordered a shrimp dish at a restaurant, and that it had something like eight shrimp in it, and he ate the whole thing, enjoyed it, and only got the mildest of tingles in his lips from eating it.

At first, I wondered if he'd ordered a spicy dish, but he clarified and said that tingling in his lips and mouth was one of his symptoms. I became alarmed, but took a deep breath and said, that's OK, at least you aren't likely to be so allergic as to have an anaphylactic reaction. He asked me what that was, and I told him the symptoms. I told him about people who died as a result of smelling something they were allergic to. I said he probably didn't get reactions just by smelling. He paused too long, and he said, actually, he did get reactions in the past when people were eating shrimp near him in a restaurant and the smell traveled to him. I nearly fell over. I asked him to clarify his allergy, and it turned out shrimp was it, not seafood in general. We had cleared seafood, but not shrimp particularly, so in that session, we cleared remaining shrimp issues, and I told him he probably shouldn't eat shrimp regardless, because what he had described to me was a potentially life-threatening allergic response to shrimp. He had eaten a bunch with almost no reaction, which proves the clearing process worked, but was something I would never have encouraged if I had realized all the facts.

So, this clearing procedure works, even on dangerous allergies, but don't take chances after doing the clearing. If you have a life-threatening allergy, avoid the substance, but even in that case, a clearing might prevent a reaction when you unintentionally are exposed, as in a restaurant situation, or for example, if you are allergic to bees but don't have an epipen with you when you get stung.

This procedure involves dowsing to find out about past lives that are contributing to the allergy and then clearing energies as needed. It requires a level of intuition that is higher than normal and goes beyond dowsing unless you make up a complicated bunch of charts with all possibilities on them, which most people do not have. Note: SRT (Spiritual Response Therapy) practitioners can use their charts for this.

Step 1: Are Past Lives A Factor?

This is a vital step, because past lives are not always a significant factor in allergies, but if you get a 'yes' to this question, proceed through the other steps.

Are past, parallel, future or other lifetimes contributing to my allergy or sensitivity to _____(insert name of substance)?

If you get a 'yes', continue. If you get a 'no', stop here.

On a scale of 0 to 10, with 8 or greater meaning other lifetimes are a significant factor in causing or exacerbating my allergy or sensitivity to

_____, *how much are other lifetimes contributing to my allergy/sensitivity?*

If you get 8 or higher, proceed. If the number is lower, it's a judgment call. A 3 or less probably is not worth pursuing, but 4-7 is up to you. It can't hurt to clear past life energies, and it doesn't take that long.

Step 2: How Many Lives Are Involved?

If other lifetimes are a significant issue, ask how many are contributing, because it may be more than one.

How many other lifetimes are contributing to my allergy/sensitivity to _____?

You can use a chart or just name numbers in order or ask if the answer is less than 5, then narrow it down further. Whatever works for you. Make a note of the number. Go to Step 3.

Step 3: Do You Need To Know The Facts?

You don't always need to details of a past life in order to clear the energies. Ask the following question:

Do I need to know the details of any of these lifetimes in order to clear the energy completely and permanently?

You will get a 'yes' answer if hearing the details is important to clearing the energy. If you get a 'no', skip to Step 5. If you get a 'yes', ask this question:

How many lifetimes do I need to get details for in order to clear the energies completely?

Usually, you won't have to get details for more than 1 or 2 lifetimes. Go to Step 4.

Step 4: What Are The Details?

For each lifetime that you require details, do the following procedure and make notes of your results. You may change these questions, add more or do whatever works best for you to get details. We find that tuning in to the question often yields intuitive responses that give entire pictures of that lifetime, and you can dowse how accurate those impressions are. The questions that might prompt the details you need include:

When did this life occur? Past? Parallel? Future? Then get a date by asking a series of questions, like:

(For past lives) How long ago was it? Less than a hundred years ago? Less than a thousand? Just go incrementally until you get a ballpark. You don't need the exact date, just a time frame for your mind to latch onto.

Was I human? Male? Female? If not human, you need to ask about what type of animal, plant or spirit in general you were. Again, you don't have to be too specific, but you do need a general idea, as that will tune you in and help you get further details.

At any point in the process, you can ask:

Are these enough details to successfully clear the allergy energy at this time? Keep dowsing until you get a 'yes' answer.

What was my major role in that lifetime that affected my current allergy? Wife? Mother? Priestess? Farmer? See what your intuition offers. You may have been a fisherman if you have a seafood allergy. You may have been a rancher or farmer if you have a dairy or meat allergy. A failed business or death as a result of your career, business or role in life often leads to allergies.

How did I die? If not by natural causes, it is likely due to whatever is triggering your allergy. If you were killed by a tiger, you may be allergic to cats in this life. If you died in a fire from smoke inhalation, you may be allergic to smoke. You may have died by disease, suicide, been murdered or killed in a revolution. Often, your death ties in to the allergy.

If you died of natural causes, check this:

Did someone I love die as a result of my business/career/status/experience? Sometimes, the death of a loved one is just as traumatic as your own death. For example, if you were a housewife, and you put up some preserves, and they got contaminated and killed your family, but not you, you may have an allergy to that food as a result.

Usually, it's understanding the cause of death and tying that in to the current allergy that completes the research. When you feel you have enough, ask the question:

Are these enough details to successfully clear the allergy energy at this time? Keep dowsing until you get a 'yes' answer, then move on to Step 5.

Step 5: Clear The Energies

This part is actually easy as long as you can power intention. The goal is to focus on the energies of that lifetime that contributed to the current allergy and transform them completely using a statement of intent like:

Please disconnect me energetically from that lifetime and transform the energies of that lifetime to beneficial for me, quickly, easily, comfortably, safely and permanently.

Repeat for each lifetime you must clear.

Step 6: Verify Results

Confirm your results by either dowsing your level of allergy/sensitivity to that substance now, or by using a question that asks if you have completely and permanently cleared the energies contributing to or causing your allergy or sensitivity.

What To Do After A Clearing

Allergies don't have to be forever. Nigel had a longstanding cheese allergy, and I a lifetime dairy allergy that were both cured in one SRT (Spiritual Response Therapy) session that ferreted out past life causes and then cleared the energies. In fact, never see a physical condition as a permanent aspect of who you are. Allergies can be resolved, and in many cases, you will be able to live normally and even safely ingest or be exposed to what were once allergens. However, this healing can take time and involve a number of steps.

If you have food allergies, by all means clear the past lives involved, but then restore your liver to top function and check yourself for leaky gut, as that is a root cause of many allergies related to food. Healing the inflammation in the gut and restoring the gut flora to proper balance will go a long way towards healing the allergies. If you don't feel competent to deal with something this complex, find a holistic practitioner who is and work with her.

If you have allergies to inhaled substances, think about what those allergies mean. Pollen allergies could mean you have beliefs that nature is out to get you, or that life on earth is not safe, something along those lines. Work on clearing those beliefs.

If you are allergic to chemicals and manmade substances, you may have beliefs that humans are dangerous and are poisoning the planet, and that you are powerless to stop them and must be a victim of their stupidity or venality. Work on a new perception so that you are not a victim of the stupid things people do.

We have found that best results are obtained when you do something to support physical healing as well as doing energy clearing work, so go to the section on diet and try to optimize your diet, and also check out your organs/systems and optimize their function.

Finding Root Causes

YOU CAN USE health dowsing to select remedies and methods that will erase unpleasant symptoms, but if you ignore the root causes of those symptoms, the energy usually will manifest in other ways later on. In addition, if you don't deal with what is causing the symptom, the issue often becomes stronger and harder to deal with in its next incarnation. For this reason, we advocate discovering root causes and healing them as the best way to experience optimal health.

What is a root cause? You might think the root cause of the rashes you get every time you eat strawberries is an allergy to strawberries. In a sense, the allergy is the physical root cause of your symptoms. But is it the ultimate root cause?

Remember that earlier we said that all ill health begins as an imbalance or problem in the energy body. In the case of your strawberry allergy, you may physically need to mend your liver and balance your immune response and heal your digestion, but it is likely that the root cause is a past life trauma that needs to be cleared. This is often the case with allergies.

If you do some dowsing about your low energy level, you may discover a vitamin or mineral deficiency or a toxicity problem. Such things would be the physical root cause. Certainly, addressing them will help resolve the condition. But why did you get a toxic reaction or deficiency in the first place? Physically, it may be due to some contaminant in your environment or diet, or a poor eating plan that doesn't give you all you need for optimal health. But why did you have those experiences in the first place? Is there an energetic root cause for those situations? The answer is yes. There is an energetic reason you were exposed to toxins or eat a poor diet. Often, beliefs or energies are a fundamental issue in this type of situation, for example, the belief that you cannot and will not be nourished by this life on earth. Another possible root cause is weak energetic boundaries, because a poorly-functioning immune system is often a sign of boundary issues.

When you spend time trying to uncover the energetic root cause of your health challenges, you will begin to see how important energy is to creating wellness. You will also see the benefit of doing ongoing energy work to strengthen and balance yourself.

We can't give you an instant understanding of the complexities of dealing with root causes, but we can show you an approach that will give you a chance to develop your own skills and get more and more out of health dowsing.

Physical Root Causes

The proximate cause of most health issues is a physical root cause. Sadly, conventional medicine often fails to even look for the physical root cause. Allergies are a good example. There are plenty of medicines for suppressing allergic reactions, and that is what many doctors turn to as a solution. As my doctor told me back in 1990, it's too hard to figure out what's going on with allergies, and you might as well just take an antihistamine (he suggested Seldane). The problem with that is the drug doesn't fix the root cause of your problem, and since histamine has many jobs, blocking it can have unwanted side effects. Instead of fixing things, you just got another problem you'll have to deal with down the road.

As a health dowser, you have the skill to reveal the physical root cause of your situation. **You can use the 'General Checkup List'** earlier in this chapter to home in on possible causes by asking how much each thing is contributing to the condition or symptoms you are experiencing. This is a slight modification of the general purpose of the protocol, which is to show you levels of certain things overall, so that you can work to keep them minimized. But you can use the same protocol to see how much, for example, toxicity is contributing to your current set of symptoms. That is a different question from the overall level of toxicity on your body at this time. You can adapt a protocol from a general to a specific inquiry in this fashion.

You can use the results of the 'Organ/Systems' checkup to point you in the direction of physical causes, as well. If your toxicity number is moderate to high and your liver tests low, that indicates that you need to work on detoxing and liver support. Getting all your systems functioning well will aid your overall health and help you eliminate symptoms by solving physical imbalances and problems.

You can also dowse a list of common minerals and vitamins to see if you are seriously imbalanced on any. Here's a question that would work:

On a +10 to -10 scale, with -1 to +1 being balanced, what is the level of _____(name the vitamin or mineral) in my body at this time?

A high positive number indicates too much, while a big negative number indicates a huge deficiency. Try to confirm results before investing in a supplement program, and we always recommend a healthy diet—food—as the number one way to balance vitamins and minerals, and if you still have issues, then a good multivitamin and mineral supplement rather than supplementing just one thing.

Vitamins and minerals are very complicated, and you should not load up on a single one in most cases. For example, most people are taking way too much calcium, which requires vitamins K2, D and A to work, but they are not supplementing those vitamins, so the calcium piles up in the wrong places in the body (soft tissues instead of bones), leading to illness and even death. Loading up on calcium also tends to deplete magnesium, a vital mineral.

Here's another thing to think about. Your dowsing might indicate your calcium level is +5, and that makes sense, since you are taking a calcium supplement, but that doesn't mean the calcium in your system is being used properly. In fact, it may be making you ill. So just having a certain amount in your body is not always a guarantee that a mineral or vitamin is being utilized or absorbed well. Your calcium level could dowse as 0 (meaning balanced), but that is not a guarantee you are OK. With vitamin and mineral deficiencies, the first things to examine are your eating plan and your digestion. If you balance those two things, you will rectify a lot of problems. There are more interactions and complications about vitamins and minerals than doctors are aware of, so use the above question as a starting point only. And be sure to dowse your diet and digestion as well.

This example is intended to help you get a feel for how complex health is. When you dowse and get a single physical factor as a root cause, it is likely you are only seeing the tip of the iceberg. Be prepared to deal with multiple things in the course of correcting a condition, and don't expect overnight success from addressing a single issue. We don't want to discourage you, but it's wise to have a realistic picture of the complexity of the human body's function so that you don't lose heart or give up when things take more time than you'd like.

Energetic Root Causes

We like to address physical imbalances and root causes, but we always try to identify and resolve the energetic root cause as well, because illness begins in the energy body. 'Energy' is a vague and all-encompassing term, so it is wise to spend a little time discussing energies that affect your health.

There is energy in your environment, and it has been scientifically proven to affect your health and well-being. Space clearing is a way of harmonizing those environmental energies to create good health. There are many types of environmental energies, and this is not a book on that subject, but you need to be aware of the variety of energies that affect your health. There are noxious earth energies, often referred to as geopathic stress. Manmade energies that are harmful include curses, non-native EMFs and human discarnates (ghosts). Cosmic noxious energies can come from stars, non terrestrial entities or even aliens. Environmental energy can be the root cause of your issue, and the protocols in the 'Environmental

Energies' section of the this chapter will help you evaluate your environment.

Not all energy is outside of your body. Your personal energy is internal, a result of your emotions and beliefs, the programming you have and patterns you inherited from your parents and their parents. Trauma is a huge contributing factor to negative personal energies like faulty beliefs and negative emotions. These detrimental internal energies manifest as bodily symptoms, so that if you are alert, you may take measures to rebalance and restore harmony, thereby restoring health.

There are a number of good books available that help you interpret the messages your body is sending when you have a certain symptom, and those references are useful in treating the energetic root cause of your issue. In fact, these books are the first thing we go to so that we can identify the true root cause and work on it. You don't need dowsing for this, but you do need one or more of these books which tell you what symptoms mean energetically. See the Resources section for titles we've used.

One nice thing about this approach is you can address root causes without being a good dowser. All you need is to identify the symptom, go to the reference guide and find out the energetic cause, then treat it using whatever method you like best. You can also choose to just work on the energetic root causes, but we have found it more effective to address both physical and energetic at the same time.

One caution is that when you refer to a book that lists possible energetic causes, especially if it is an abbreviated book, your energetic cause may not be listed. Use your intuition and be open to hearing the truth as you read the list of possible energies. Be detached. The correct energy will resonate with you.

As you become more used to self-evaluation, it will become easier to pick out the energy that you are reflecting. If you simply are not sure which among the choices is correct, you can dowse which one most resonates with you or which one is closest to the root energetic cause of your symptom. If none seem to apply at all, consult a bigger book or look online for further interpretations.

Summary

If you resolve physical and energetic root causes of your symptom or condition, you will see healing. It is most effective if you work on both the physical and energy bodies. You can use many of the protocols in this chapter to identify those root causes, and a good starting point for interpreting symptoms (even for non-dowsers) is to have one or more books that will point out the energies of symptoms.

Identifying root causes is a complex process, and you can approach it in many ways. What follows is just one possible routine to use. You can construct your own once you have some experience.

For Physical Causes

To find the physical root cause or causes, you can use the 'General Checkup List' and 'Checking Organs/Systems' protocols in this chapter. A question you can adapt to those lists is:

On a scale of 0 to 10, with 0 meaning no effect and 10 being 100% of the root cause, what is the effect of _____(name an item in the list, as in an organ or system, or inflammation or toxicity) on my current symptom(s)?

Anything 3 or under is very mild. An 8 or higher indicates a significant contributing factor. If you want to go with percentages, you can add them up until you get 100%. Or you can go with the numbers representing intensity rather than percentages, in which case, your answer will show how strong a factor is, not what percent of the cause it is.

For Energetic Causes

To discover the energetic root cause or causes, you can evaluate aura, chakras, beliefs and environmental energies and then drill down to find the specific issue.

On a scale of 0 to 10, with 0 meaning no effect and 10 being very strong, what is the effect of _____ (enter an item from the list, for example, environmental energies) on my current symptom(s)?

You can use dowsing to determine whether you have found all the significant factors, and then find a method or modality that will resolve that root cause.

∼

Aura & Chakras

CHAKRAS

My mother, who was never a believer in energy work or dowsing, once complained to me that her left arm had been giving her bad pain for a long time, yet she had no recollection of having injured it. She wasn't the kind who would go to a doctor, and she was so sick of the pain that she was willing to try anything I suggested. My first thought was to check the chakras in her arm. When a chakra is shut down, energetic 'pressure' can back up behind where the flow of energy is blocked, leading to the perception of pain. If there is pain that comes out of nowhere and there is no history of trauma, the chakras are a good place to start.

I had a similar thing happen when I lived in the UK, where there was a line of negative energy running in front of the sofa we used to sit on each night for a few hours. Eventually, that negative line of energy caused my foot chakras to shut down, leading to bad pain that nearly made it impossible for me to walk. The excruciating pain went away quickly if I opened the chakras, but the chakras would later shut down again, because I kept being exposed to that negative line. Finally, we dowsed about the cause and discovered it was environmental energy. When we did a space clearing, the line went away, and my foot chakras never gave me further trouble.

In my Mom's case, I dowsed devicelessly and discovered that my mother's elbow chakra was closed. I did that by pointing at each joint in her arm, starting at the shoulder, where the pain was worst, and moving down the arm to the wrist and hand, and asking:

On a scale of 0 to 10, with 0 being closed and 10 being optimally open for her, what is the level of function of this chakra (the one I was pointing at)?

The problem could have been any of the chakras in any joint of that arm or hand, but only the elbow chakra gave me a 0. I told her to visualize along with me and see that chakra opening in slow motion like a flower bud to the appropriate level of opening for its function at that time. (You don't always want it fully open, though that might seem to be best. Just ask for optimal function for that person at that time.)

As soon as we completed the visualization, the pain in my Mom's arm disappeared, and it never came back. I didn't dowse to find out why the chakra had shut down, because the pain didn't come back. So you see, chakra issues like this may be one time deals or a result of an ongoing energy assault. Just being able to dowse and reopen chakras using intention and a visualization is a simple, effective way to solve pain issues in some cases. (Note: dowsing does not fix the chakra. Intention and visualization do.)

Aura

Your aura is the energy field of your subtle energy body, and it extends well beyond the physical body. It can have damage just like your physical body can, and repairing that damage can resolve physical symptoms just like opening closed chakras does. The results may not be as dramatic, but they can be measurable.

Dowsing is an excellent way to evaluate the function of your aura and chakras and determine the best ways to repair them. Since

Barbara Brennan's book *Hands Of Light* goes into extraordinary detail on the use of pendulum dowsing for these things, we refer you to her book for details. Balancing and repairing your aura and chakras are useful regular activities for creating good physical, mental and emotional health. Even a beginning health dowser can usually get good results when dowsing about auras and chakras.

Subconscious Beliefs

CONSCIOUS BELIEFS ARE what you would say you believe in. They may even be a foundation for your code of ethics or the way you live. Subconscious beliefs exist in your subconscious, deep below the conscious level, and are not accessible by rational thought.

Your subconscious is tasked with keeping you alive. Survival is its priority. Your conscious mind charts your course through life, at least, when you are living consciously, which is not that often. Problems occur when your conscious and subconscious agendas are in conflict.

Since it takes a lot of practice and effort to live consciously, most of the time, our actions are controlled by our subconscious. We live our lives on autopilot, not really thinking that hard or asking a lot of questions. When you live subconsciously, as all of us do most of the time, your subconscious beliefs are in charge. Your conscious beliefs are only in charge when you are living consciously.

Your conscious beliefs often conflict with your subconscious beliefs, and that means the subconscious wins, because it is in charge most of the time. People wonder why their lives don't unfold the way they consciously desire, but most people are not aware of the importance of living consciously. Only when you are living consciously can your conscious beliefs assert themselves. Even then, because survival is a body's number one priority, they can still be overridden if they conflict with a subconscious survival belief. A survival belief can relate to physical, emotional or spiritual survival of yourself or those you love.

We have a colleague who says there is only one real and true belief, and that is the belief that "I am Pure Spirit, and I can experience anything I want." All other beliefs are faulty. This is an excellent way of looking at the situation. Why can't you just get rid of 'bad' beliefs and keep the good ones? Because it has been demonstrated that over time, beliefs can change. One of the weakest and most replaceable words in a belief is 'not' or similar words. We have seen beliefs that started out as "I must not lie" become "I must lie" simply because the 'not' is lost. Alternatively, we have also seen a 'not' get added into an original belief and change its meaning completely. This illustrates that beliefs have no permanence as 'good' or 'bad', so none of them is really helping you.

The average person has lots and lots of faulty beliefs. They are created at times of trauma in this life and past lives. They are imprinted by programming from parents, religion, employers, society and family members. And over time, words can be replaced or altered in ways that completely change the original meaning.

It is not (in our opinion) a good investment of your time to commit to ridding yourself of all faulty belief codes. We spent a long time learning how to discover and clear them, and we worked for years with clients. We have come to the conclusion that it isn't wise to focus a lot of time on 'what's wrong' with you, as if you have to clear it all in order to achieve your goals. We doubt a person could ever completely clear all the belief codes they have, and even if you did, others would pop or activate as you moved through life.

Our approach is to clear beliefs that are having a significant effect on a situation so that you can spend more time doing things to create positive outcomes than chasing down things that are self-sabotage or working against you. So try not to make clearing beliefs a crusade. Just use it when they are a significant cause of your issue.

Beliefs have a tremendous effect on your health and life in general, but how can you know what they are? The definition of subconscious beliefs is that they are not reachable by your conscious mind, so that makes it sound impossible to discover them. However, there are two ways that we know of for revealing subconscious beliefs. The hard way is to learn to observe what is going on in your life, some pattern that you don't like, and then backtrack to a belief that describes that pattern. The easier way is to dowse.

Interpreting A Pattern

An example of a negative pattern would be that every time you manage to save money, an unexpected expense comes along and wipes your savings out. Now, think about beliefs that could cause this pattern to be expressed. Some possibilities that describe it well are:

- I must not save money.
- Every time I save money, I have to spend it.
- I am not able to save money.
- I don't want to save money.
- It's not safe for me to save money.

These beliefs would directly cause the pattern observed. There are other beliefs that would allow that pattern to develop that are not directly related to the pattern. Here are some examples:

- Rich people are greedy.
- Rich people are selfish and evil.
- I hate rich people.
- Rich people get killed by robbers.
- I must not be greedy and selfish.
- Saving money will make me rich.
- If I am rich, I will go to hell.
- I am not powerful enough to become wealthy.

Any of the above would support a pattern like the one described. Your subconscious wants to keep you alive, but it also doesn't want an emotional or spiritual death or trauma. When you begin to save, it consults the rule book and discovers that you don't want to be like rich people or that you think rich people are more likely to be killed by robbers or go to hell.

A trauma in a past life can create a very strong belief. For example, if you were rich in a past life and a mob killed you, as you died you might have thought, "If only I hadn't been rich, I wouldn't have been killed." That becomes a belief, "Rich people get killed by mobs." Therefore, you will never be rich.

The same thing happens with health issues. You can have direct beliefs that instruct you to be ill in some fashion, or you can have indirect beliefs that prevent your enjoying perfect health. Let's say the pattern you have seen is that you have never been strong and fit in your life, but instead are weak and sickly. Here are some direct beliefs that could cause that:

- I must not be strong.
- Strong people are abusive.
- It is masculine to be strong. (This will be detrimental if you are a woman.)
- Strong people cannot be gentle.
- I must be gentle.
- It is dangerous to be strong.
- Strong people hurt others.

Some beliefs that could indirectly contribute to the pattern would be:

- I must not be powerful.
- Powerful people abuse their power.
- Power is dangerous.
- Strength is power.

This last belief could be called an equivalency. Equivalencies are beliefs that define words incorrectly. In other words, they make your system think they are equal, but at the conscious level, you know they are not. It still doesn't matter, because your subconscious is in charge.

An equivalency we have seen a lot is sick=love. We need to explain the secondary benefits of bad experiences so you can understand why you don't want this type of mechanism active in your system. What is a secondary benefit? If there is any positive aspect to your having the negative experience, and that positive is very important to you at the conscious or subconscious level, you will continue to experience the negative. Sickly people sometimes are ill because for them, a secondary benefit of illness is they get attention they would not get otherwise, and love is very important. Or else, being ill has the benefit of giving them 'permission' to have 'me' time, and their system realizes unless they get time to repair, they will become ill or die. If illness is a longstanding issue for you, check to see if you have the subconscious belief that sick=love. If so, you will be sick often, as love is important to us. Or check to see if you subconsciously or consciously believe that you are not allowed to take time for yourself unless you are sick.

Now, you can tell that many of the beliefs listed so far are wrong or silly, while others sound reasonable. The more reasonable they sound, the more likely you are to have that belief at the conscious level as well as the subconscious, which means it will be harder to clear. Subconscious beliefs can be tough, but it's even harder to change faulty beliefs if you agree with them. An example would be if you say that you do consciously believe earth is a terrible place, that you don't belong and that you don't feel safe here. This will affect your health.

Dowsing Subconscious Beliefs

Observing a pattern and guessing the beliefs behind them works, but it takes time and effort. Dowsing is the easiest (and only other) way we know for revealing subconscious beliefs. It's easy to use dowsing to find out what your subconscious believes. Just ask.

On the subconscious level, do I believe that_____(state belief)?

You must be detached, because many of these beliefs are downright stupid, and most of us don't like to think we are dumb. But we all have silly beliefs, and the sooner you discover them, the better.

Beliefs generally revolve around survival, power and choice. Many beliefs follow certain word patterns, like:

I must not_____ (put what you want to experience in the blank)

I must_____(put your symptom or condition in this blank)

It is unsafe for me to_____(put your goal in the blank)

I am not able to_____ (put your goal in the blank)

I will die if I_____ (put your goal in the blank)

You can state your health goals in a concise sentence, then use any of the above phrases to test if you have subconscious beliefs that are in conflict. Just put your goal into the blank (except for the "I must" statement).

You can use dowsing to check overall subconscious beliefs about health or to check for beliefs that are affecting a certain condition or symptom. (You can, of course, use this same protocol to check for subconscious beliefs that are blocking you in any area of life).

When you discover a faulty belief, you can usually transform the energy with a statement of intention, such as:

Please transform the energy of this belief quickly, easily, comfortably, safely and permanently.

Then go back and see if the belief is still true at the subconscious level. It should not be, if you have powered your intention. If you cannot power intention, then use another clearing method to get rid of it.

Another reason a belief may not clear is that there is a belief 'propping it up' that needs to be cleared as well. This creates a further layer of complexity that is best discussed in an advanced course on belief clearing.

Dowsing about and clearing beliefs is the topic of courses and books, and this book is not a course in beliefs, so we suggest that you do further research on this topic and get more training if it resonates with you. Even at the beginning and intermediate level, you can do a lot of good belief work that will help your health, but advanced training will make the process easier.

Environmental Energies

ENVIRONMENTAL ENERGIES HAVE BEEN PROVEN to cause ill health. Scientific studies have mostly revolved around what is called geopathic stress, or noxious earth energies. While geopathic stress is an unconventional concept, people have been aware of detrimental earth energies for thousands of years and used that knowledge to avoid living in places that contributed to ill health.

Environmental energies can be detrimental or beneficial to your health, and there are many types of them. Some of them are not conventionally recognized as potentially harming your health, like curse energy and alien energy or entities. Others, like manmade EMFs, have been subjected to quite a few studies that show they are harmful.

Your goal is to live and work in safe, healthy locations. The two places most critical to that goal are where you work and where you sleep, as those are the two places you spend the most time. If those two places are harmonious and supportive of health, you are going to be in much better shape than the average person.

You can create harmonious, salubrious space to live and work in. Space clearing is the method that we use. Feng shui is an ancient Oriental method for accomplishing the same outcome. We find space clearing adapts best to modern challenges. Either method will improve the energy in your environment. If you don't want to do it yourself, you can hire a professional, but it is wise to educate yourself in the basics of environmental energy so you can hire someone who really knows what they are doing.

Even if you are not a dowser, there is much you can do to harmonize your space and make it healthier. Here are some steps to take:

Step 1: Choose Wisely

Where you choose to live and work is the most important choice you can make, because once you are settled somewhere, you might feel stuck, even if you aren't. It is far better to pick a harmonious, healthy place than to try and leave a bad one. Even if you can't dowse, you can 'feel' the energy of a place. Healthy locations feel harmonious and peaceful and lovely and quiet. Unhealthy places feel sharp and agitated and sometimes even scary. Do not spend much time in places that feel bad, as they probably have detrimental energies.

Many people have beliefs tied to money and power that say they don't have choices, but the fact is, we all have choices. You may choose to become a lawyer and apply for a high-powered job in a busy city, or you may not feel particularly in tune with a college education, and you drift into a minimum-wage job in a toxic neighborhood. Your work space is probably harmful in both cases, and your living space could be equally bad. Living in a poor, decaying neighborhood is a prescription for encountering noxious energies. But living in a fancy place might end up harming your health just as much if it makes you feel tied to a job that is toxic to your health. It can be very hard to give up nice things, even if they are not healthy in the long run.

Most of us make poor choices and from them learn what we would prefer instead. Don't beat yourself up, and do not feel trapped. Look hard at your situation and make choices to release toxic people, jobs and locations, and ask the Universe to support you in finding a harmonious situation.

In the meantime, use space clearing and feng shui techniques to create the most harmony you can at home and work. Put your intention to live in safe, healthy space out there by showing you are committed. That will lead to doors opening for you to make it easier to achieve your goals.

Your apartment or home can be an oasis in a sea of toxic energy. It will take effort, but it can be done. You will at some point decide moving to a healthy location is preferable, even if it means giving up some conveniences. Just take it one step at a time. Go to Step 2.

Step 2: Improve & Maintain Healthy Energy

No matter where you live and work, set goals about your health and do your best to maintain healthy energy in your environment. Doing regular space clearing is a must. Use feng shui techniques, too. Many are simple and affordable. Keep your space clean and free of clutter. Surround yourself with objects that reflect your commitment to health, whether in the form of healthy plants, an aquarium with beautiful fish or pictures showing places that remind you of happiness and good health.

Manmade EMFs are one of the most harmful factors affecting health at this time. Wifi, smart phones and appliances, smart meters and cell towers are just some of the EMFs that will erode your health. Dirty electricity is another. The nice thing is that there are meters for measuring the levels of EMFs at home and work, and there are professionals who offer this service if you don't want to do it yourself.

Make sure you don't have dirty electricity present. Dirty electricity is when you have frequencies other than the normal 60 Hz coming through on your electric lines. Other frequencies piggyback on the lines, and these frequencies can create nasty symptoms in sensitive people.

Eliminate sources of wifi by converting to ethernet and discarding smart appliances, phones and limiting your exposure to blue light from computer and other screens. Do yourself a favor and get rid of manmade EMFs as much as possible. Even if you cannot dowse, this will help improve your health.

What if you live in an area where other people's EMFs spill into your space? This is most common at work or if you live in a high density area. Shielding from outside EMFs is much harder and more expensive to do than controlling your own environment, and for that reason, we urge you to consider living and working in situations that are healthy rather than putting yourself into challenging ones. Such a choice, as in Step 1, can be tough to make, as you may perceive you have to give up things you are attached to. Or maybe you tell yourself you don't have the money. Try to avoid feeling powerless. Take whatever action you can.

Once you have done the best you can in your current situation, then it is time to go to Step 3.

Step 3: Re-evaluate Your Goals & Make Changes As Appropriate

Whatever choices you have made in the past and whatever actions you have taken to create a safe and healthy environment, revisit those choices periodically to make sure you still resonate with them. Maybe you finally get tired of being owned by your possessions and doing a job you hate just to pay the bills. Perhaps it's time to simplify your life. This could be a hard choice if you have family and they are not all on board, but your health and theirs should be your first priority.

What if you are on the other end of the spectrum, feeling powerless to leave a decaying neighborhood for lack of funds. You know that it is too hard to maintain safe and healthy space where you are, but you aren't sure how to move on. You don't have a lot of possessions that 'own' you, but you are still trapped due to money, in this case, the lack of it rather than attachment to what it buys. Your biggest challenge will be to believe you can make a change, that you deserve to live somewhere safe, and that the Universe will support that choice.

Whether you are rich and stuck or poor and stuck, getting unstuck is best done by self-work that shifts your energy to believe that you have the right to choose your life and that there is a path that will get you where you want to go safely without punishing you. We do personal energy work almost daily, and we recommend that you do the same. If you want to change your circumstances, whether for health or money, you must change your energy, because your beliefs and energy are what create your experience. You understand the power of subconscious beliefs now, and most of us have a lot of faulty subconscious beliefs that interfere with our ability to choose what we really want. Doing belief work may be the best choice for your goals. On the other hand, maybe clearing emotional trauma would be better. Dowsing can help you choose a therapy for your goals.

Bottom line, your environment is a reflection of your energy in some fashion, and if you want a healthy life experience, you need to create a healthy environment. Start with your bedroom and your workspace and try to expand beyond that, but do look at overall changes that will help make it easier for you to create harmony and happiness in your living and work space, as that will lead to improved health.

Dowsing Environmental Energies

Your environment is probably changing rapidly, so it behooves you to use dowsing to determine the effects of environmental energy on you, especially since energy is invisible. You can ask this question for any space that you spend time in.

On a scale of +10 to -10, with 0 being neutral and negative numbers being detrimental, what is the overall level in effects on my health and well-being of the environmental energies present at _____(fill in the location)?

You can ask about your entire property, your bedroom, your bed, your desk or office at work, the local grocery store or mall, your favorite bookshop or library. If you get a -8 or worse, you really need to do a clearing on that space for your own needs. Get a professional or learn to do it yourself, and then check the energies afterwards. We have books on space clearing if you want to learn how.

Because energy is dynamic, you need to check energies regularly and clear them as needed. A -3 or less is a minor effect, but -8 or worse is highly detrimental to health. Use your judgment about how often to clear based on what answer you get to the above question. We have found that monthly clearing at work and quarterly clearing at home are the minimum for most locations. Work usually needs more frequent clearing, because of higher traffic and greater stress, but if you are having a lot of stress at home, you may find it necessary to clear more often there. Dowsing will guide you.

∼

Choosing Modalities, Remedies & Therapies

NOTE: In this section, we are assuming that you have already decided you don't need a doctor for your condition or symptom. If you aren't totally sure, consult the 'Do You Need A Doctor?' section.

This section is meant for situations that you intend to handle yourself, or in conjunction with a holistic method you are familiar with. If you are working with a doctor already about this issue, your time is best spent going to the next section, 'Evaluating Side Effects', where we will show you how to use dowsing to determine the level of side effects of what your doctor recommends. If you just want to evaluate the efficacy of what your doctor recommends, you can use this question:

On a scale of +10 to -10, with 0 being neutral and negative numbers being detrimental to my health goals, what is the overall level in effects of _____(insert the therapy or suggestion your doctor made), done as and when my doctor recommends?

Ideally, you would want to get a +8 or higher before you proceed. It is wisest to do this dowsing at the time the doctor suggests it, so you can ask for other options if you get a bad number.

The rest of this section is aimed at times when you have dowsed you can do a better job using methods you know, and you want to sketch out a program that will give you the best results.

Many people who take up health dowsing do so because they have a specific condition they want to heal. This book can be a valuable tool in your healing process, but you need to learn how to approach health dowsing to get the best results. We've tried to help you step back, ask yourself what health means to you and to consider that health is far more complex than any of us can imagine. Medical science is still in its infancy, as much as it would have you think otherwise, and there are myriad factors that significantly affect health which conventional medicine knows little or nothing about.

By helping you create a bigger, more flexible picture of what health is and how to create it, we hope to empower you to resolve any health issue or symptom: your own, a family member's, a pet's or a client's, using the same basic approach.

It doesn't matter if you are trying to get rid of migraines or cure food allergies or just want to have more energy. By stepping back and looking at the big picture, you can follow the same basic approach, no matter what your symptom or condition.

We take the time to repeat that here, because there is a tendency for people to think that your approach will vary depending on the ailment. They ask how to use health dowsing to fix a food allergy, and then they'll ask how to use health dowsing to handle recurring skin rashes. It doesn't really matter what symptom or condition you have, the basic approach will be the same. When you understand that, you have simplified your approach to health dowsing, and that will build confidence and success as well as streamline the process.

Step 1: Something Seems To Be Wrong (Skip if you already have a test result or diagnosis)

If you have a persistent symptom, or you did your monthly organ checkup or system check and got a number you didn't like, the first thing you must do is to determine if the cause of what you are experiencing is good or bad for you in the long run. Consult the 'Good Or Bad?' section in this chapter and dowse to determine the answer.

Your next step is fundamentally different depending on your answer. If the process driving the symptom is positive in the long run, all you need to do is support the process rather than suppress it. (You can go to Step 3 and modify the questions if you want to dowse how to support the process.) If the process is detrimental, go to Step 2 to move towards a solution.

Step 2: Find The Root Cause (optional but recommended)

You can skip to Step 3 and find a fix, but knowing what the root cause is will give you more choices and a better feel for the situation. Use the 'Finding Root Causes' section in this chapter to uncover the root cause or causes.

Step 3: Select A Solution

This 'Choosing Modalities' section may be everyone's favorite, but jumping ahead to a fix is taking short cuts, which is why we have repeated the full process in short form before showing you how to take this very important and satisfying step.

You are a unique person, and your health goals are specific to you. In the 'What Is Health?' chapter, you spent time working to define health and sort out your health goals. You now understand they include any factor that influences your choices. For example, money is a factor for most people. Time is a factor. Your concept of your level of intelligence and competence may be a factor. The tools you have in your healing toolkit or the therapists you know are a factor.

We are assuming you did the work in the previous chapters and have considered your current goals and priorities, as well as your viewpoint on health, conventional or holistic. In other words, you aren't simply looking for something that will heal you; you are seeking something that meets your needs and desires and resonates with your energy, because that will work best.

You should by now also have a list of methods, modalities and remedies you are willing to pay for or have in your toolkit. You can make a chart or just list dowse. Always include the word 'other' in any list or chart to show you understand any list is potentially incomplete.

For purposes of this section, think of 'remedy' as relating to something you take, like a herb or supplement or flower essence, while 'modality' or 'therapy' is something you do or hire someone to do, like Reiki or reflexology.

Are any of the methods on this list (on this chart) an 8 or higher on a scale of 0 to 10, meaning they are good to excellent, for resolving the root cause of my current condition/symptom, considering my overall health goals and priorities?

Technically, this question is not necessary if you put 'other' on your list, but it's good to ask directly if the best solution is on your list. If you get 'yes', then you can dowse which solution. But if you get 'no', then you need to step back and either add to your list or maybe reconsider seeking outside help for your problem.

There are a number of ways to find the best solution on your list. You could ask if there are any that are 10 on a scale of 10, or you can ask which one ranks the highest, and then dowse what the ranking is on a scale of 10. The goal is to find out which item gives you the highest number for your goals, whatever those are.

What item is the highest ranking method on this list on a scale of 0 to 10, with 10 being best, for resolving the root cause of my health situation (or name the symptom or condition) given my overall goals and priorities?

You can replace the 'goals' phrase with an actual list of your demands, if you wish. Or you can ask this question individually for each priority you have. For example, you can ask which method will have the fastest results with the lowest side effects, you can ask which one will cost the least, and so on. As you can imagine, it is likely that if you dowse about just one priority at a time, you will get different answers to different questions, which will inform you about each item on your list. You can then ask the question overall, knowing this information.

Another wrinkle is you can ask about physical root causes separately from energetic root causes, so that you can work with both to get faster healing. Just make little changes to your questions to address the specific information you are looking for and be very clear about how you define terms.

Maybe using more than one method at a time will be more effective than using just one. Here is a question for determining that:

Would using more than one item on this list give better overall results for my goals than simply using one?

If you get 'yes', then ask:

How many items used together will give me the best results? 2? 3? And so on…

When you get the number, say, 2, then assign names Item 1 and Item 2 to represent the two methods that are best, and ask:

Which item is Item 1?

Which item is Item 2?

Then test the two together to make sure you got it right.

What is the overall level in effects on a scale of 10 of using Items 1 and 2 simultaneously to achieve my goals?

The number you get should be at least as high as the number of the highest ranking you got for the individual items. For example, if you got an 8 for Item 1 and a 9 for Item 2, anything less than a 9 for using them together means it isn't a good idea, because you are diluting the effects. Ideally, your number for using both should be higher than using either alone. That proves that the combination is more powerful than either one alone. So in this case, a 10 would show that using them together was indeed a good choice. We personally don't invest in solutions that rank below an 8 on a scale of 10.

Now you need to figure out how to apply that solution or solutions. Go to Step 4 if you got one remedy. Go to Step 4a if you got one modality or therapy. Go to Step 4b if you got more than one solution of any kind.

Step 4: How To Apply The Solution (1 remedy)

If you got that a remedy like a flower essence or homeopathic or supplement or herb is your best solution, you still need to figure out dosage and frequency. That is, how much and how often to use it. You can use whatever they say on the label, but you are unique. You may do better with less than recommended, or you may need more. (Never use a lot more than recommended of anything without a doctor's order, as that can lead to toxicity issues.) Dowsing is the best way to determine the perfect dosage and frequency for you.

Frequency

You can use a question like this for frequency:

Considering all my goals and priorities, what is the best dosage to use of this remedy?

Take it more than once a day?

Take it once a day?

Take it every other day?

Take it every third day?

Is the best frequency the one recommended on the label?

Use your judgment to craft questions that will ferret out the best frequency. You might ask, "How can I get an accurate answer about frequency without determining dosage (or vice versa)?" This is one of those weird dowsing situations where it works out fine. You can't dowse two things at the same time, so pick whichever makes sense to you, trusting that the second set of answers will match. In any case, at the end, you are going to confirm your answers.

Dosage

Assuming again that this is a pill or liquid of some type that you are ingesting, ask about the dosage.

What is the most effective dosage for my goals, taken _____ (fill in the frequency you just dowsed, for example, once a day)? One pill? Two pills?

You can substitute volume measures for number of pills, or you can use measures like 1/4 tsp for loose solids. You can even use weight measures.

For How Long?

Lastly, you need to determine how long is the optimal time of treatment by this remedy or method.

For best results, how long should I take this remedy _____(insert dosage and frequency)? More than a week? More than two weeks?

For infections and acute situations, the time will usually be shorter than for longstanding conditions where you are doing natural and gentle solutions.

Note: One of the most important things to hold in your focus is your desire to have side effects be zero or very minimal, in other words, for this remedy to work gently, safely and comfortably. It is too easy to allow one's eagerness for healing to overcome caution with respect to side effects. It is far better to take longer to heal without side effects than to experience bad side effects.

Confirm Your Dowsing

Once you have determined what you think is the optimal dosage, frequency and duration, dowse how effective that exact combination will be on a scale of 0 to 10 for your goals.

On a scale of 0 to 10, with 8 or higher being good for my goals overall, how is _____(insert dosage, frequency & duration, such as 'taking 2 _____pills every 8 hours for 7 days')?

If you get less than an 8, something is wrong. Go back and retest and get a new regimen and then confirm. In the event that you keep getting 'wrong' answers, you are probably being told by your intuition that you are barking up the wrong tree. Step back, start over and look at the big picture. Your dowsing sometimes will go wonky to let you know you are going in the wrong direction.

Step 4a: How To Apply The Solution (1 therapy or modality)

If you have healing methods on your list, the questions you ask may be slightly different if you get a therapy or modality as your best solution. Some modalities will be ones you can do yourself; others will require a professional you know. In both cases, you need to determine how often and how long to do the therapy for best results.

This is true whether you are talking about Reiki, acupuncture, The Emotion Code, EFT or reflexology.

Assuming you have identified the best modality, now you can ask how many treatments it will take to reach your goals (this is like dosage for a remedy):

How many _____(insert modality) treatments will be required for best results for my goals?

You can just name numbers in order, or ask 'less than 5?' or whatever you like to find out how many treatments are best.

Once you have that number, you can sort out how often to get them (frequency):

What is the best frequency of _____treatments for my goals? Daily? Weekly? Monthly?

Bear in mind that a treatment you can do yourself costs nothing but time and effort, and you might dowse that you need to do it often, while considering your budget, you might get a lower frequency for something that requires a professional, such as acupuncture.

Some methods shift a lot of energy, although that is somewhat dependent on the patient. Don't push the frequency because you are impatient to see results. You need time to process, to release energy, to let energies transform and to release toxins in some cases, and rushing will cause side effects. As a rule of thumb, only do one type of treatment in any 24-hour period to avoid side effects.

For How Long?

As with remedies, you need to determine how long to continue the treatment. You don't want to waste money and time, but you also don't want to stop too soon.

For best results, how long should I continue _____(treatment and schedule)? More than a month? More than two months? (Test whatever time period you like).

Confirm Your Dowsing

When you believe you have obtained the optimal schedule, dowse to confirm your results:

On a scale of 0 to 10, with 8 or higher being good for my goals overall, how is _____ (insert schedule, such as 'one acupuncture treatment a week for a month')?

Step 4b: How To Apply The Solution (2 items from your list)

If you have a list that includes both remedies and therapies, there is a chance you will dowse you need more than one thing. In that case, use questions as from Step 4 and Step 4a for each individual method, and then confirm the combined schedule for efficacy. Also be sure to check whether it is most effective for your goals to do the multiple things simultaneously or sequentially.

Evaluating Side Effects

WHAT DO we mean when we use the phrase 'side effects'? A side effect is an unintended consequence of an action you take to improve your health. You can get a side effect from just about anything. Here are some examples:

- Your body gets achy from a new exercise program
- You get a detox reaction from doing a cleanse
- There is a die-off of yeast or bad bacteria when you try to restore your intestinal flora to a good balance
- You experience an allergic reaction to a drug or herb
- You feel fatigued after a treatment like Reiki or reflexology
- You have an allergic reaction to the dye they inject you with for doing medical imagery
- You have nightmares the night of an energy treatment, or you feel a negative emotion you can't explain

- The general anesthetic used for your surgery causes an allergic reaction or overtaxes your liver
- The new diet you are on seems to make you less energetic
- You have insomnia since you went on a certain drug
- There are unexplained aches and pains since you started taking a prescribed medicine

In general, we talk about side effects being negative and unwanted. Sometimes the side effects are expected or at least not too surprising, because research has shown they might happen. When you are taking steps to improve your health, minimizing the side effects is a high priority. You want to feel better from what you are doing, not worse. A certain amount of discomfort may be necessary, as in a detox or rebalancing, but it is desirable to allow change to occur at a slow enough pace that your body can resolve these challenges easily and discomfort does not go on for a very long time.

Side effects can often be reduced if you drink plenty of pure water and give your body extra rest during the process. Don't do too much, too fast. Impatience for fast change leads to more side effects as the body rushes to keep up with the changes.

Dowsing is an excellent tool for predicting side effects from any change you make for your health. Regardless of what you are testing, the protocol is pretty much the same. You are using a 0 to 10 scale to measure the intensity of any side effects, so that you can prepare, or if necessary, switch to another method to avoid them.

Side effects can be devastating or minor. Obviously, minor ones are just a nuisance, but dowsing allows you to make choices that minimize all the side effects, which will make life much smoother. If I had been able to dowse for health back in the early 1990s, I could have avoided a devastating reaction to the general anesthesia used for my second knee surgery. That reaction debilitated me completely, as it crashed my liver. It took me about eight weeks to recover enough to live a barely normal existence, but the aftermath of the liver damage affected me horribly for a few years until I was finally able to get it fixed. Conventional medicine offered no solutions, and the symptoms were rather challenging and unpleasant. Had I been able to dowse, I would have known that the surgery was going to have a negative outcome. I could have chosen not to have it, or I could have dowsed in detail what about the procedure was dangerous for me. But I wasn't a dowser at that time.

Dowsing will help you avoid dangerous side effects that can cripple or kill you. A certain percentage of people die from prescription drugs every year. You don't have to be one of them. Likewise, a number of people have adverse reactions during surgery, either to anesthesia, the procedure itself or an accident. With dowsing, you will be much less likely to experience any of those things. Even the most natural remedy can have adverse reactions in a small percentage of people. If you happen to be highly allergic to a particular herb, avoiding it could save your life.

We have harped on how dowsing for health allows you to customize your health choices to your unique needs. Nowhere is this more valuable than in determining possible side effects of proposed medicines, surgery, remedies and therapies. We all read about horrible side effects to using certain drugs and procedures, yet the doctor will pooh-pooh your concerns, saying only a small percent of people have a bad reaction, as if you couldn't possibly be in the minority who get hurt. How can your doctor be sure that you aren't the one person in one hundred or a thousand who will have a bad reaction? The only way to know for sure is to dowse. Otherwise, it's like playing Russian roulette with your health.

This is one dowsing activity that may save your life, the life of a family member or a beloved pet, so practice this protocol any time you get a chance, and refine your technique and hone your accuracy. You'll be glad you did.

This protocol can be used to test many things. Here is a partial list:

- Therapies, both holistic and conventional
- Drugs
- Surgery
- Herbs
- Supplements
- Procedures like MRIs and scans
- Diets
- Exercise programs

Anything that you anticipate doing to improve your health might have a side effect. Dowsing will tell you if there will be one, and how intense it will be. A sample dowsing question for this purpose is:

On a scale of 0 to 10, with 0 being no effect and 10 being death, what is the level of side effects of _____ (insert the proposed action, including details like when, with whom and what brand as appropriate) on my overall health and well-being?

Why would you include the surgeon's name for a procedure and an approximate date? Because the surgeon is a variable, as is the timing. Perhaps you would have a good outcome with one surgeon, but not with another. Or maybe that surgeon is great, but that time frame is either not optimal for your body or there may be a massive blackout that day during surgery, or the surgeon gets sick and someone stands in for him or that day, or he'll be all upset and unable to focus. The more variables you include in your question, the more reliable the answer.

One brand of supplement might have binders or additives that you are allergic to. A particular antibiotic might be a formula that you react to, while another antibiotic is fine. The dye used in imaging might cause an allergic reaction, or the timing of your acupuncture session might lead to more side effects than if you picked another date for the treatment.

For us, anything 3 or under is not dangerous, though a 3 usually indicates a noticeable reaction. If you get a 4-7 answer, that is a moderate level of side effects and could be unpleasant. If you get 8 or higher, it could mean a very bad reaction. For example, think of all the people who have had adverse reactions to vaccinations, reactions that totally ruined their lives. Dowsing can help you avoid that kind of problem, if you become an accurate dowser. Next to the 'Do You Need A Doctor?' question, this particular protocol offers you the most potential benefit to your health, so practice it often.

We encourage you to use a journal and write down questions and answers and refer back to it to confirm your results after the fact. You may find that a 4 is not an unpleasant level of side effects for you. Or you might find that a 2 is about as high as you wish to go. You are unique, so fine tune what you do for your specific body.

If you get a very high number, don't be afraid to get a second opinion or have a dowser you trust check your answer. But also do not be afraid to follow through with what your dowsing has told you. This is one big reason we urge you to build a team you can communicate with. If you get that a drug your doctor is recommending is going to have side effects at a 9, and you are afraid to ask him to offer you another, your dowsing has not helped you at all. It has locked you in to believing you will have a bad outcome. This is totally counterproductive. Do not attempt to dowse side effects if you are unwilling to take right action based on your dowsing.

8

DOWSING FOR YOURSELF

Creating A Regimen

A regimen is a plan that is designed to give a positive outcome. You can create a regimen for any health goal. You might want to become stronger and more fit, or have more energy, or sleep better, or resolve the cause of a condition that is bothering you. Dowsing is a good way to put an effective plan together.

Step 1: Be Clear About Your Goal

First, you need to identify a specific goal. Revisit the section on setting health goals in the 'What Is Health?' chapter. Your goal needs to be positive, not negative. For example, losing weight is a negative goal, yet it is very common. Think of what you intend to create, not what you want to eliminate. You may find it difficult to put into words why you want to weigh less or how you will feel at your perfect weight or what you want instead of the problems you perceive excess weight creates, but you must take the time to figure out what you want, because negative goals are problematic in many ways.

The goal also needs to be measurable and in your mind obtainable. You also need to be committed completely to doing whatever it takes to succeed. This last factor is vital.

In our years of working with clients, the one consistent truth about successful cases had to do with the client being so fed up with their situation that they were totally committed to changing it. Sometimes, it seems that it is that laser-focused intent that brings results more than any particular method you could use.

Step 2: Select Your Approach

If you have a goal like becoming more fit, you're clear that you are striking out for that result, and it isn't confusing. But what if you are working on a health problem or symptom? If you have a symptom you want to be rid of, your first have to discover whether that symptom is a sign of a dis-ease condition or a sign of something that is positive in the long run, like a detox or transformation. Refer to the section 'Good Or Bad?' in the chapter on 'Dowsing Protocols' to refresh your memory about how to determine whether the unpleasant symptom you have is in the long run good or bad for your health.

A symptom you have had for a very long time is usually a sign of an imbalance of some kind, and is therefore not good for you. The imbalance or toxicity needs to be addressed. Symptoms that are more recent can be confusing, because they may be unpleasant, but only dowsing can identify whether they are something you need to be concerned about or just support.

If your regimen is to treat or resolve the root cause of a symptom, be sure you have dowsed whether the cause of that symptom or symptoms is good or bad for your health in the long run. In both cases, you can create a regimen to follow. For 'good' processes, you support the process rather than stop it, and you can attempt to make it smoother. For 'bad' processes, you need to address the root cause so that balance can be restored.

Step 3: Do You Need A Professional?

If you can tell your situation is a simple one that you can handle, fine. Or if you know you should go to the Emergency Room, do that. If you aren't sure whether this is something you can do on your own with the tools you have in your toolkit, then use the material in the previous section to dowse whether or not you need to consult with a doctor. When in doubt, make an appointment. If you get that you don't need outside assistance, go to the next step.

Step 4: Dowse What To Use

If you are dealing with a dis-ease process that you have dowsed you can resolve, you will be looking at applying a remedy that will resolve the cause of the problem. If you are trying to support a positive process, you want a method which will allow it to continue, but do so more smoothly and comfortably for you.

Conventional medicine assumes all symptoms are bad and should be eradicated, but remember the section on messages from your body? Killing the messenger does not help your health. So with health dowsing, you determine what the message is, and then you can dowse how to improve things. (It's true that you can theoretically use dowsing to find the best way to suppress a symptom, but that won't give you the best long-term results.)

If you have a dis-ease process, get your list of potential remedies and healing methods and dowse which one or ones are most effective for your goals. An example of a list you might have is:

- Homeopathics
- Flower remedies
- Reiki
- Tapping
- Herbs
- Symbols
- Colors

- Supplements

Or you can also have a list of methods for helping you reach fitness goals, and they might look a bit different.

- Change in diet, example: cut out sugar or add good fats
- Types of exercise, from walking to yoga to weight lifting
- Drink more water
- Eliminating blue light sources
- Supplements that help that goal, such as those for the immune system or digestion

You can see that the items in the list may vary a little bit depending on your goal, but don't get tunnel vision. We have found that sometimes, unexpected activities and methods dowse as great for a goal. For example, tai chi might dowse better for building your strength than weight lifting, but if you don't put it on the list, you won't know that. So think in very broad terms and be willing to be surprised.

For something longstanding, it is possible that making a big change in your life would be the most therapeutic thing to do. Some examples could be:

- Move to a new location
- Divorce your spouse
- Get a new job
- Identify what you are passionate about and pursue it
- Adopt a more positive outlook
- Reduce stress significantly

Most of these things are not going to be easy to do, but if any of these resolves the root cause of your issue, dowsing will confirm that making the big change is the best choice for reaching your goals. What good will taking a supplement or getting a treatment do if the stress from your job is making you ill?

The same question can be asked to evaluate any of the above in terms of their effect on your health goals. Something like this would work:

On a scale of +10 to -10, with 0 being no help but no harm and negative numbers being detrimental, how useful for my health goals would _____be?

More than likely, multiple items will test high. Make a list of those that are +8 or higher. Then test them all together.

As a health regimen that I perform regularly, how would _____(list all the items) be for fulfilling my health goals on a scale of +10 to -10, with +8 or higher being of significant assistance?

If you make a list of items that all test +8 or better, hopefully when you test them together, they are still +8, and it would be better if the number were higher. If it is less than +8, that means the combination is not a good one for your regimen. You can try dowsing combinations, removing one item, to see which one is detracting from the score, or if it is just one item.

You will need to set up how often you do each item, and the dosage, if the item is a remedy like a herb or homeopathic. Check the 'Choosing Modalities' section in the previous chapter for how to do that. When you have dowsed how often and how much to use of each item, re-dowse the entire regimen again, inserting not only the methods, but their dosage and frequency. You can use the above question, replacing 'regularly' with the dosage and frequency of each item.

As long as the number you get is +8 or higher, you can then proceed to use the regimen. If not, you will need to do further work to determine why the number is low. It may be that the frequency should be changed if you combine items, so try altering that and re-evaluating.

If you are experiencing a positive process that is uncomfortable, dowse your available list of methods for supporting the process. Some of the things you use for dis-ease can be helpful here, as well. A sample list is:

- Symbols
- Colors
- Flower remedies
- Drink more water
- Clay (good for detoxification)
- Herbs
- Supplements
- Charcoal (good for detoxification)

Since you are unique, we don't know what tools you will have. Obviously, the more tools you have, the better.

Your dowsing question will pinpoint which method or methods will best support the process. A sample question is:

On a scale of 0 to 10, with 8 or higher being significantly helpful for making this process smoother, easier and more comfortable, how does _____(insert the method) rank?

Sometimes you'll find that something as simple as drinking more water or getting more sleep will rank very high. Be imaginative and make sure 'Other' is on any list or chart of methods you dowse. For details, see the end of this section.

While physical remedies are often very helpful, remember that energy is the root cause, and a true healing or rebalancing usually requires a shift in energy. Subtle energy medicine is powerful, and if you want to be preventive, proactive and maintain good health, we suggest you learn all you can about this topic, and add a healing or energy clearing method to your list of possible methods.

Step 5: Dosage, Delivery & Frequency & For How Long?

Once you have dowsed the therapy or remedy that will work best for your goals, you need to determine how to deliver it, how much to use, how often and for how long. Dowsing will help you pin down these important details. You can use the questions in the 'Choosing Modalities' section in the previous chapter as templates for this purpose.

Step 6: Check Your Regimen

As your healing proceeds or your health improves, the regimen you are using will probably become less effective, because it was conceived for helping you when you were different energetically and physically. For that reason, we recommend you dowse the effectiveness of any regimen at least monthly and make changes as needed to make sure what you are doing is at least an 8 on a scale of 10. Also, keeping a journal of what you do and your progress will help you to stay focused on your goals and to know when it's time to make a change in your regimen.

What If You Get 'Other'?

Beginning dowsers or those who are feeling a lack of self-confidence about their knowledge base with respect to health are going to be afraid of getting 'other' when they dowse, because that answer requires them to do some digging. The more you know and the more experienced you are, the easier it will be. Conversely, the less you know and the more of a newbie dowser you are, the harder it will seem.

If you are afraid of getting a certain answer, it will impact your dowsing accuracy. Remember, being detached is vital for dowsing accuracy, and that means being willing to get whatever the answer is. If you are borrowing trouble about what you're going to do if you get 'Other' as your answer, you will probably not dowse accurately. So relax and try to realize that even if you have no idea what to do, it's OK. You are still miles ahead of people who aren't dowsers. If you cannot achieve a good level of detachment, that's a sign that you probably shouldn't be dowsing about this question.

What you do when you get 'Other' as an answer will depend a lot on what question you were asking. One thing is for certain. You will be challenged to think outside the box, meaning to think in new ways for you. Try to see this as an opportunity to grow and expand your perspective. It isn't a test.

Sometimes it will be fairly easy to sleuth out the answer. If you are dowsing for a modality or a remedy and don't get one on your list, instead getting 'Other', just add more. Maybe you left acupuncture off the list, or herbs. Relax and take a deep breath and ask to be shown the best answer for your goals. If necessary, do a little search online to get a bigger list of remedies or therapies.

If you are dowsing among categories you have been given, that can pose a bigger challenge. For example, we told you that we categorize environmental energies by source as earth (geopathic), manmade or cosmic. These are made-up categories, so they are not necessarily perfect or all-inclusive. In fact, in recent years we have occasionally come across a noxious environmental energy that tests as 'Other'. What we found was that these energies shared factors from more than one category, so weren't an exact fit for any of the three we had. An example would be an energy that involved both alien and human energies, thus being both manmade and cosmic. When something like that happens, you might want to rethink your categories and update how you define them, or add a new category.

Sometimes when you get 'Other', it might mean to shift your thought pattern. Maybe you are thinking it's either go to the doctor or do it yourself. Perhaps the way you are looking at it as either/or is not best in this case. Maybe for your goals, doing both in a certain way is going to give better results.

Don't let the 'Other' category disturb or frighten you. It is a wonderful opportunity to expand your thought process and dowsing skill.

Messages From The Body

IF YOU BELIEVE as we (and many others do) that ill health begins in the subtle energy body and left untreated, manifests in the physical body, then it makes sense that when you have a symptom, it's a message from your body about what is out of whack energetically as well as physically. How do you treat the messages your body sends? What do you do when your phone rings? Do you take a hammer to it to shut it up? Of course not. You answer it, because it may be important. For the same reason, it is wise to pay attention to the messages from your body.

Conventional medicine aims to eradicate the symptom, which is foolish in many ways, but especially self-defeating if you regard physical symptoms as messages about your body needing help. If you treat the symptoms as messages and you try to understand and respond appropriately to them, you can more easily create the health you want, because you aren't waiting for things to get bad. You respond when you get the first message.

Paying attention and interpreting and responding to your body's messages (symptoms) is a key part of our approach to health. It is a totally different approach than most people are used to, but it is a cornerstone of preventive maintenance, so if you are willing to work on prevention, this is a tack you should take.

There are many good books that interpret your body's symptoms so that you can rebalance energy and resolve the cause of them. We have listed our favorites in the Resources section, and we suggest you invest in the best one your budget will afford.

An interesting fact about the messages is that they aren't about diseases; they are about emotions, trauma and beliefs. What this means is that the root cause of a disease isn't physical. It's energetic. Often you are out of harmony with good health because of patterns from your childhood, programming from your culture or trauma you have experienced in the past. By transforming these energies, you can restore your body to greater balance and allow good health.

Because you will be dealing with nonphysical causes, you need methods for transforming emotional energies and beliefs. We have found EFT (Emotional Freedom Technique) to be excellent, but The Emotion Code and other methods also work. You cannot experience good health if you are overcome with negative emotions. Negative emotions signal you are off the path to happiness and fulfillment, and that opens you to ill health.

Here is the basic process we use when we have a symptom that lasts more than a day or two:

Step 1: What Is The Message?

Look up the symptom in your reference books. The book *Messages From The Body* (see the Resources section) is our favorite and the most complete of the bunch, but it is also the most expensive.

Step 2: Treat The Cause

Use your favorite method to transform that energy of that symptom or heal that trauma.

Step 3: Evaluate Results

Watch for results. If the symptom goes away, that is a good sign. If not, you may have missed something. Some situations are complex, and others are longstanding and have taken hold in the physical body, and thus will benefit from physical treatment and support as well as energetic healing.

This system is best for problems that are new rather than longstanding. For stubborn issues you have had for years, you will need a multifaceted approach for best results. This protocol is best for preventing dis-ease from developing by nipping it in the bud. It is also useful for discovering the root cause of longstanding problems, but you need to be aware that resolving them will most likely take time and effort.

Where does health dowsing fit in? You don't really need to be a dowser to use this protocol, but if you are given a list of five possible energetic causes for your symptom and you aren't completely sure which one is correct, you can dowse to find out. You can also use dowsing to pick the most effective way to shift the energy. We feel this approach is so valuable that we wanted to share it with you, even though it isn't necessary to dowse in order to benefit from it.

Creating Your Health Team

FREEDOM OF HEALTH care choice has been eroded in the last 50 years to the point that you may feel you don't have a choice anymore who your health care professional is. You may not have the freedom to choose what doctor you work with, if you are part of the conventional system. If you don't have the money to go the holistic route, you may feel stuck. Your best bet is to immediately institute self-care of a preventive nature. Become a good health dowser so you don't need to use the system often. It may take you a long time to achieve this goal, so get started now.

Even if you are older and don't see a financial way to see holistic doctors regularly, you can still implement a lot of what we recommend in this book to avoid being sucked into the black hole of the health care system.

Choices Within Your Insurance Plan

Even if your choices are limited, dowsing will help you make good ones. If you require a specialist to consult with, hopefully you will be given a choice, and if so, dowsing will help you make a good one. As always, you need to be very clear on your goals before you create a dowsing question.

You might assume that because you are getting a referral, that you trust the doctor is correct in recommending it. But if you have any doubts or strange feelings about following through, that is another reason to dowse. What if the doctor is wrong, and you don't need a heart specialist? Is it a good thing to be subjected to all those tests and stress if it isn't needed? Dowsing is a good way to decide if you want to follow through on a doctor's recommendation, and if it doesn't dowse well, then you can find a way to get a second opinion, hopefully from someone who has a different perspective.

Here is a potential question if you are in a situation like that:

On a 0-10 scale, with 8 or above being very accurate, how accurate is Dr. _____'s assessment of my need for a consultation with a _____(list the type of doctor) for my current health goals and challenge?

If you don't get an 8 or above, you probably don't need to go that route. Remember, he's just following procedure, and his decision may be excellent, or it may not reflect your condition or needs.

If you feel good about the referral, but you have a choice between two doctors, both covered by your plan, then you can dowse the following:

Considering my health goals, on a scale of 0-10, with 8 or higher being good, how beneficial overall would consulting Dr. _____ be for my current health challenge?

This question does not evaluate the intelligence or integrity of the doctor as such, though those things would be a factor. It is aimed at telling you whether that doctor can effectively help you reach your goals. Can you see why it's important that you are clear and specific about your goals? Your goals should include not only the health outcome you want, but also factors like how easy or comfortable you want it to be, how expensive of time and pain, how few side effects, etc.

Your Health Team

For those who have the money and freedom to create a health team, dowsing is a wonderful way to build it. You are unique, so we can't tell you exactly what professionals you need to add to your team. That's where using your rational mind and dowsing come in.

Sit down and look at your health goals you created in an earlier chapter. Make a list of health challenges you've had for the longest time. Try not to assign a disease name. Instead, be broad. Digestive challenges, autoimmune issues, weak bones are examples of what to list. You don't want to identify with a disease as such.

Think about what you and doctors have done to help cure your conditions. If they aren't cured, if only symptoms are being addressed, then ask yourself if you are satisfied with that approach. Have you accumulated a ton of prescriptions because of all the side effects of the meds? Are you better off than you were when you asked for help? If not, a new approach is called for. Or is it just that your doctor is close-minded and has a bad attitude? Maybe a new doctor is what you need.

Whether you are switching from conventional to holistic or you are just creating a new team within your belief system, dowsing will help you. If you are going the allopathic route, variations on the questions in the previous section may be used to help you find a new doctor on your plan who will be in alignment with your goals and preferences.

If you are going holistic, answer the following questions. What do you want to experience? What system or organ seems to need help? What types of holistic practitioners are you familiar with? A chiropractor could be a good doctor if you are trying to overcome structural issues due to an accident. A naturopath might help you if you have digestive or immune issues. You might want to get regular massage therapy, Reiki or Jin Shin Jyutsu treatments, because they have helped in the past. Oriental medicine or acupuncture might be attractive to you, even though you don't understand it. There are so many systems. You will benefit from doing some online research to find out what the methods and values of systems are.

Perhaps you want to address a single issue at first. Dowse which type of practitioner will be the most help in resolving the cause of your issue significantly, if he or she cannot cure it. You may sequentially go through different professionals, or you might overlap treatments, or you can put together an entire team to cover all the bases. It's up to you and your budget. You can use either a 0-10 scale or a +10 to -10 scale. Here's a sample question for a particular condition:

On a scale of 0-10, with 8 or higher being good to excellent, how would working with a _____(name the type of method, like chiropractor) be for helping me to resolve the root cause of_____(list the condition)?

You can even add a phrase at the end of that question (such as 'given my personal preferences') that indicates your preferences in a general way, if you have a time frame in mind or a budget or want a certain kind of relationship.

Multiple Team Members

You can dowse which of these is best for you, to add a professional one at a time, giving each method some time to work, or consulting more than one during one time period, because they complement each other. It is not uncommon to have more than one doctor or health care professional help you, but make sure that your team are all in alignment not only with your outlook on health, but with each other.

It can create friction and be ineffective if you hire two doctors for the same purpose. Avoid creating conflicts wherever possible. Only hire complementary help as needed.

Another issue is that if you are seeing a conventional doctor but then go to a holistic doctor or energy worker, you will usually get conflicting information, because the approaches are totally different and in most cases, not compatible. Conventional medicine relies on drugs and surgery, while energy and holistic medicine prefer gentle and natural approaches. It is very hard to combine the two opposing viewpoints and get success. This is why we suggest you decide which camp you are in for a given purpose, and then stick with it. Only switch camps when you are sure it's time for a new approach. Don't use a scattergun approach thinking the more different things you do, the better your chances. This isn't gambling; it's your health, and you need to have a clear viewpoint. Any approach can work, but you need to believe in it and commit to it. So give your favorite approach a chance.

We can't give you a stepwise approach to creating your team, because your needs are unique. Whether you add one professional at a time when it becomes clear you need the added help, or you construct a multi-person team at the start, depends on your needs and your unique situation. Dowsing can help you decide which is best.

Don't Do Too Much At One Time

As a rule, you don't want to do more than one treatment per day. Going too fast will give you side effects. However, years ago I went against that and got a massage before my chiropractic adjustment, because my muscles tended to be tight, and it seemed to make the adjustment easier. Use your judgment and dowsing, but normally do only one treatment in a given day.

Working With Your Doctor

ASSUMING you have chosen to be active in your own health program and that you have put together a team of professionals whom you trust, then you are in an excellent position to create good health. You are in charge of daily maintenance and prevention and for discovering how to take care of simple issues. When you are presented with a puzzle you can't solve or an acute condition, you turn to your team and get whatever help is needed. They are also indispensable when working on health problems you've had for years that are too complex for you to unravel.

It is assumed that your team will listen to you about what you dowse and what you intuitively feel and give you the respect you deserve for being an active participant in your health care. If you are slighted or ignored by your doctor, or if your doctor sneers at you for believing in dowsing, that doctor is not going to be a useful team member.

You are the one who has the most to lose or gain, and you have a right to participate and be heard. Arrogance is not a substitute for intelligence or effective treatment and should not be tolerated, unless there is also integrity, intelligence and effectiveness. Your goal is to find health care professionals who will allow you to participate to the extent you wish, who will listen to you, respect your opinion and do their best to explain their opinions to you.

This all seems so self-evident to us, but we often hear from clients that their doctor fired them or made fun of them for having a differing opinion. We've even had a client say the doctor yelled at her for not wanting to take a certain drug. Others have told us that they disagreed with the doctor or had an intuitive hit or dowsed that what the doctor suggested wasn't a good thing, but they were so intimidated, they never spoke up.

The conventional medical system doesn't have a monopoly on arrogance, but it tends to foster such behavior by pressuring doctors to spend less and less time with patients and push questionable drugs and surgeries on them as the best (or only) solution. This means they don't really have time to convince you or explain much, plus they are way out of date in their understanding, as the minute they leave school, it becomes harder and harder to stay current in their field.

Your conventional doctor may be a very nice person who wants to do well, but in the current system, he doesn't get paid to listen; he gets paid to sell. When you won't buy his viewpoint immediately, you slow down the process and in a sense question his intelligence and motives, even though that is not your intention. Your resistance becomes an obstacle to his success and self-image. An example is how doctors are now paid bonuses for having their patients vaccinated. This creates a real conflict of interest between you and your doctor if you don't see eye to eye.

The bottom line is put together a team you are comfortable with and who allow your input. It doesn't matter whether you go the conventional or holistic route, as long as you do this. You don't really need to be able to dowse to accomplish this, because so much of it is just common sense. Don't enter into relationships where you are treated badly.

9

DOWSING FOR OTHERS

Professional Or Not?

Helping others by using health dowsing can be very fulfilling, and you can either offer it as a free service or charge for it. Be sure to familiarize yourself with laws relating to health and healing services in your area before you invest in a business.

We suggest that you learn your craft and give yourself a time of apprenticeship so that you can become masterful. You can help friends and family during this time and accept no payment. Keep a journal of what you do and learn from your experiences.

When you feel you have mastered the most important aspects of health dowsing, then you can hang out your shingle. It is wise to check the market in your area for such a service and what the going rate might be. Health dowsing is not yet a common method, and if you are trying to create a full-time income, you would be smart to combine it with some other service, like a well-known healing therapy or modality. For example, if you are an accomplished Reiki practitioner or Bowen therapist, you can combine health dowsing with what you offer, increasing the ways you can help people and thus increasing your income potential.

Health dowsing also would be an asset if you are any kind of health care professional, conventional or holistic. Your recommendations and diagnoses will be more effective if you add health dowsing to your methods. You wouldn't necessarily have to inform people you were using health dowsing in such a case; you could use your judgment. There would be no ethical considerations, since you would only be dowsing for patients who had asked for your help.

Maybe you aren't interested in making money or don't want to get involved in creating a business model or doing marketing. In that case, you can still share health dowsing with friends and family. The most important person you can use health dowsing for is yourself, and if you do that, you are making a contribution to the world.

Permission & Ethics

PERMISSION IS REQUIRED before you dowse about another person. By permission, we mean actual, verbal agreement to allow you to dowse about that person or their pet. Dowsing is a very powerful tool, and like any power, you need to wield it ethically. Since dowsing delves into personal matters that are not your business, you must obtain permission before health dowsing for others.

You might ask why, if you are trying to help someone become healthier, would you have to have their permission? Think of it this way. Maybe you smoke or drink alcohol or eat the occasional junk food. How would you feel if a friend or family member barged into your home without permission and rifled through your cabinets and closets and threw out things they felt were injurious to your health? That would be a violation of your privacy, regardless of their intention.

Your intentions may be what you consider 'good,' but you have no right to tap a person's phone, eavesdrop, snoop or dowse about them without their permission, regardless of your motives. It's that simple. Be an ethical dowser and only dowse for those who request your help.

What about health dowsing for an animal or child? You can get permission from the parent or caretaker, but then it would still be wise to dowse if the person or animal is willing to allow you to dowse about them. If you get 'no' for an answer, do not dowse.

Animals

HEALTH DOWSING for pets can save you a lot of money, and if you are a professional, it can also provide you with income. We have used health dowsing for our many pets over the years, and it has saved us thousands of dollars in vet fees and helped us get faster, better outcomes. And that's something all pet owners would love.

You can adapt the 'Do You Need A Doctor?' protocol in the 'Dowsing Protocols' chapter to decide if going to the vet is a good idea in a given situation. You'll need to formulate your personal goals first. Think about your budget. Sad as it is, you may not have the funds to go beyond a certain expense to help your pet. If that is the case, include that in your goals. How competent are you with natural remedies and therapies? The more tools you have in your toolkit, the more likely you are to feel comfortable treating your pet's problem yourself.

Other factors to consider are if the vet would have a quicker and more comfortable solution for your pet; if what your vet would suggest or do would have very negative side effects; if you don't have a method that would resolve the issue, but the vet does. You can see why it's best to think about this well before you need to dowse, and even write it down so that as you change, you can change your goals and your dowsing statement.

Euthanasia

Whether it's appropriate to euthanize a pet is a question that can be answered with health dowsing. As always, think about all the factors that matter before you ask the question. You want your pet to have quality of life. You want to do what your pet wants as much as possible. You may have limits to what you can do to help a pet who is losing basic functions, like the ability to walk or to be housebroken. Consider all the factors that matter to you when forming a dowsing question about euthanasia. You and your pet are unique. While your vet might offer an opinion, your dowsing will be far more accurate if you can be detached and are a skillful dowser.

We have seen situations where the vet suggested putting an animal down, and holistic treatment restored the animal and gave the pet additional quality time with his family. Health dowsing can give you peace of mind that you made the right choice.

As with the 'Do You Need A Doctor?' section, you can program yourself to be dowsing a long, detailed question by using a shorter question like,

Is this the appropriate time to euthanize _____(pet's name)?

Programming that question tells your system that you want to include all the factors you wrote down or listed when you chose your goals. See the 'Do You Need A Doctor?' section for details.

Health dowsing can be adapted to pets to evaluate their diet, their water, a supplement or an exercise regimen. In other words, you can use the same dowsing protocols for animals that you do for yourself in most cases.

∼

Protection

WHOLE BOOKS HAVE BEEN WRITTEN about protection, and if you are a dowser or a healer, you would be wise to read several. The concept of protection is based on the awareness that any energy you resonate with will stick to you, and when you are working with ill or troubled people, you can become a wounded healer if you don't take care of yourself.

You are especially at risk if you are highly empathetic or have beliefs at the conscious or subconscious level that say you must feel what others feel, or you must empathize or take on other people's energies. If you were a shamanic healer in a past life, you probably took on energies to help sick people heal, and that tendency is present today, but you don't have the training to do it safely.

We suggest you use protection, but don't think it's a panacea. Protection is better than nothing, but it won't work all the time, and you are better off doing self-work to eliminate energies that can cause you harm, like faulty beliefs and negative emotions. Protection is a stopgap measure that will help you be safer than without it, but to be truly bulletproof requires you to shift a lot of energy so you don't resonate with detrimental stuff.

Before doing a health dowsing session for others, use whatever method of protection tests best for you on a scale of 0-10. Your intention is the key. You want to be protected from any detrimental energies or influences during the session, and you can use a physical object to anchor that intention. A color, symbol, prayer of intent, crystal or just about anything can help strengthen your intention to stay safe. You can also enlist the aid of angels and guides as protectors.

Protection is not usually needed when you are doing health dowsing for yourself. However, it's a good habit to get into whenever you are doing healing or energy work, especially with someone else or in a location that is not your safe space. Do not work with someone else if you cannot get protection that dowses as a 10 on a scale of 10 for the duration of the session.

Clearing Yourself After Work

NOT ONLY SHOULD you protect yourself when working with others, you should clear yourself after a session to remove any detrimental energies you might have picked up or to clear any mechanisms that activated during the session. Sometimes a statement of intention is all you need. Or you might have a ritual you do after a session to restore balance and harmony to your system. Perhaps you like to do Reiki on yourself after each session with the intention of clearing any harmful energies.

This is not a requirement when you are health dowsing for yourself, but it is highly recommended when you work with others.

Cancer Energy

CANCER ENERGY (like any energy) is contagious. We don't mean to single out cancer energy as a bugaboo, because as we said in the previous section, you can accumulate any kind of detrimental energy you resonate with, but cancer energy is prevalent and dangerous enough that we want to give it special consideration.

You can pick up cancer energy without having cancer yourself by empathizing with your friend, family member or pet who has cancer. You may not even know they have cancer. Maybe you only know they are sick. But especially if they have a diagnosis of cancer, any interaction you have may cause cancer energy to 'stick' on you.

How easy is it to pick up cancer energy? When my Mom had cancer, every time I talked on the phone with her, I picked some up, as much as 3 on a scale of 10. Even thinking about her caused me to get some cancer energy in my system. Fortunately I was aware of this risk, so I checked and transformed cancer energy frequently during that time period using a statement of intention.

Dowsing will tell you how much cancer energy you have in your system at any level (see 'General Checkup List' in the 'Dowsing Protocols' chapter). Ideally, we'd like to see it be 0 on a 0-10 scale, but anything under 1 is fine. After you use a statement of intention to transform the energy, you can dowse and see if it is gone. If not, try again. If you can't seem to eliminate it, you need to take stronger measures. Maybe you have some actual cancer cells in your system. It could be skin cancer or maybe your system defines anything precancerous as cancer. Further dowsing will help you sleuth it out.

Knowing your current level of cancer energy will help you know whether you have picked up additional cancer energy. Working with cancer victims or having one close to you will inevitably lead to your getting cancer energy if you are empathetic or emotionally involved with the person. As long as you transform the energy, it won't have a chance to manifest as cancer in your body. If you allow cancer energy to pile up in your system, eventually it may manifest as cancer.

Liability

THERE IS ALWAYS the possibility that your dowsing may be incorrect. This can set up a liability issue, and if you are dowsing professionally, we advise you to research liability insurance and see if you can get coverage that you can afford. It may or may not be possible to even get coverage for something like dowsing.

There are no methods that are guaranteed to always be right. Doctors are sometimes wrong in their diagnoses and recommendations, but they cannot be sued for that. They can only be sued for malpractice, which is a slightly different thing. In other words, if they do their best and follow accepted procedures, they are protected from lawsuits.

Unfortunately, dowsing is not a mainstream activity, and there are no accepted guidelines for how to judge 'dowsing malpractice'. Personally, I think if you are a truly masterful dowser, then karmically you are fine even if you make a 'mistake' when dowsing. But not everyone is going to feel this way, and some health dowsing is life or death, so before you choose to practice health dowsing professionally, you need to come to terms with how you would deal with those occasions when you gave advice based on your dowsing that later turned out to be 'wrong.' This is something any practitioner in health care needs to address, because sooner or later, it happens.

You can head off some issues if you are clear with your clients about what health dowsing is and what level of accuracy it has. By explaining that dowsing is a skill that you have learned to extend your intuition, but that no method is 100% accurate, you can help your clients set reasonable expectations for dowsing. Also, make sure you don't portray dowsing as a psychic thing or overstate how accurate you are. Ego can lead to a downfall. Another thing you will find beneficial is encourage clients to participate in the process. Muscle test them or get them to dowse so that they see they get the same answers you do, and if they don't, then defer to what they are getting.

Always leave the final decision of what to do with the client and warn them that dowsing is not 100% accurate, so they should get a second opinion on any major issue. This will help prevent problems.

∽

Does It Work Over Distances?

PEOPLE OFTEN ASK if you can dowse about someone who is far away. Just as with sending healing energy over a distance or clearing space over a distance, you can dowse about a place or person that is far away. The only caveat is that you must have permission if you want to dowse ethically. Space and time are no obstacle to dowsing, healing or energy transformation, because all things are energetically connected.

10

PITFALLS

Introduction

There are many things that can trip you up when you are dowsing. In this chapter we cover all the common pitfalls any dowser can encounter. These are topics that should be covered in any thorough dowsing course, but they are so important, we include them as a refresher for you.

∼

Dowsing When You Shouldn't

KNOWING when not to dowse is every bit as important as knowing how to dowse well. It is not always appropriate to dowse, and if you persist in dowsing when you shouldn't, you can create problems for yourself. Some of the situations in which you should not dowse include:

- When you are emotionally upset or feeling ill
- If you are too attached to a certain answer

- When you don't feel competent to dowse about a certain issue
- If you can't get full protection for the session you are doing on someone else or a pet
- If you want to dowse about someone else, but they have not given you verbal permission

Sometimes you can easily tell you shouldn't dowse, but you try to ignore it. If you wish to be a masterful dowser, you must know yourself well enough not to dowse if that is the best course of action. If you dowse when you should not, often, your answers will be wrong or misleading or frustrating. Rushing to dowse when you aren't protected can have bad consequences for your health. Dowsing about someone without permission creates bad karma and shows poor boundaries and a lack of ethics.

Ego will push you to dowse when you suspect you should not. Becoming a masterful dowser involves knowing when not to dowse and not being upset about it. By choosing not to dowse when it is not safe or when it is inappropriate, you will advance your dowsing ability as well as grow in dowsing wisdom.

Making Mistakes

ONE OF THE best ways to learn is by making mistakes, recognizing them and figuring out what lesson you can learn. By doing that, you turn making a mistake into a lesson. It is natural not to want to make mistakes. We aren't suggesting you should want to get wrong answers. However, dowsing is not 100% accurate for anyone, so you will benefit if you admit from the start that you will be making mistakes, and have a policy in place for how you can learn from them. If you do that, you will become more accurate over time. You can't succeed unless you are able to fail, and you can't improve if you don't learn from your mistakes.

You may find it useful to use these approaches to mistakes:

Don't beat yourself up. You're human, not perfect. No matter what the outcome, look for the learning opportunity. This may be very hard if you overextended your level of competence and feel it led to a bad outcome, but you cannot learn if you wallow in self-pity or blame.

Evaluate your dowsing question for vagueness, lack of specificity and poor word choice. Try to figure out how the answer you got was right for the question you asked, but if you had changed the question, you would have gotten a more accurate answer. This teaches you how to improve your questions. Hopefully you kept a journal and can refer to it. You can't get good answers from poor questions.

What was your emotional state and level of detachment when you dowsed? Were you feeling agitated, angry or ill? Were you in a location that didn't allow you to dowse in peace? If you keep a journal, you can note these things and later evaluate how they affected you. It can be hard to refrain from dowsing when you really want to, but wisdom comes from making good decisions about when not to dowse.

Did you give in to ego? Did you dowse about something you knew was beyond your level of competence? Did you dowse about someone without permission? Did you take short cuts in your dowsing process? These are all mistakes that come from ego, and we all need to learn to minimize ego in our dowsing.

Don't give up on health dowsing because you made a mistake. You cannot master something if you quit when you 'fail'. Even if you are not 100% accurate, health dowsing still improves your overall decision-making success, because it is not guessing. If you are using dowsing in situations we suggested, you will without a doubt improve your results, because guessing only gives you a 50-50 shot at success.

Not Taking Care Of Yourself

HEALTH DOWSING IS A POWERFUL TOOL, and if you are a compassionate or empathetic person, you will be drawn to sharing it with your family, pets and friends. Please use dowsing first and foremost to create optimal health for yourself. That is the best advertisement for health dowsing. It will also give you a chance to become masterful and confident before you offer your assistance to others.

This sounds like common sense, but too often we have seen healers and dowsers who fail to focus on their own health and end up as wounded healers, and we don't want that to happen to you.

Poor Questions

ONE OF THE most common pitfalls in any kind of dowsing is a poor question. If you have taken our course and read our book on the topic, you probably don't need to worry about this. However, you can always strive to improve your questions to eliminate vague words and lack of specificity.

A good question includes all of the following which apply: how, what, where, when, who and why.

A good question is usually long and very specific.

Avoid using vague or undefined words in your question, like 'good'. Define the terms you use clearly.

Take plenty of time to formulate your question and write it down in your journal so you can go back later as needed and evaluate it.

Poor questions come from:

- Being in a hurry and unwilling to take the time to make a good question; too eager for the answer
- Not feeling verbal enough to form a clear question
- Lacking confidence about making a good question due to lack of practice
- Being lazy and using weasel words and phrases that are undefined, like 'highest and greatest good'

Be patient. Know your limits. Take your time. Write your question down. Go back later if you feel the answer was 'wrong' and figure out how the answer was right for that question, then make a better question.

Not In A Dowsing State

THIS IS the single biggest issue with poor dowsing. Last time we surveyed, nearly 40% of dowsers on our list had not heard of the dowsing state and had no idea what it is or didn't feel confident about attaining it. This is alarming, since you can't dowse if you aren't in the dowsing state. Now, perhaps some of them get into a dowsing state without realizing it, but most of them simply lack the training and the understanding of the skill, and so when they dowse, they get answers, but they aren't dowsing. It is vital to realize that the ability to get a 'yes' or 'no' does not mean you are dowsing.

The dowsing state is an altered brain state that one must enter into in order to allow the answer to the dowsing question to come through. Our course and our book on the dowsing state will help you master this key part of the process if you are unsure of it.

Even if you understand the need for the dowsing state, you probably will need to practice a lot before you will find it easy to attain. Distractions, monkey mind and lack of focus will make it hard to get into a dowsing state. This is why at first, having a safe, quiet and harmonious space to do your health dowsing is a real must.

We recommend that you not do health dowsing until you have mastered all the basics of technique and feel confident with them. Not being able to get into a dowsing state almost always gives you the wrong answer, and you want to avoid that.

Ego

WE ALL HAVE EGOS, and the trick is not to allow it to make our choices for us. These attitudes are a sign of an ego that is out of control:

- Thinking you can't make a mistake
- Feeling superior to others
- Believing you should be allowed to dowse about anything you wish, without regard for 'ethics'
- Overestimating your experience and expertise
- Being unwilling to rely on others
- Being more concerned about being 'right' than about hearing the truth
- Fear of hearing the truth

All of us have run into these feelings. But if you want to become a masterful health dowser, you need to be very self-aware and not give in to these feelings, most of which are based on fear and lack of self-love. By rising above these attitudes, you use dowsing as a way to release fear and ego, and dowsing becomes a way of being more enlightened.

Fear

DETACHMENT IS REQUIRED for dowsing accuracy, and fear is the biggest obstacle to being detached. When you are asking about an important health issue, you may be afraid of the answer. Fear will keep you ignorant, blind you or lead you astray, but it will never help you solve problems.

We suggest you use whatever energy clearing method you like that works to release your fear. Tapping is a good method, and we use it almost every day. The Emotion Code is one we've used on occasion, and some people swear by it. Jin Shin Jyutsu has a simple method for reducing fear: you just wrap the fingers of one hand around the index finger of the other. Do that while breathing slowly and deeply, focusing only on your breathing until you feel the fear go away. Do the same with the other index finger.

Don't ask life and death dowsing questions until you are sure you are detached. If you feel fearful when you are preparing to dowse, don't dowse. Work slowly to build confidence, asking harder questions only after you feel competent at your current dowsing level.

Don't be in a rush. Mastery takes time, and dowsing is a wonderful practice for teaching you to release fear. Dowsing will give you valuable information that will allow you to more easily and effectively respond to any health challenge, so there is no need to fear. It is better to know than not to know. If you know, you can act appropriately.

Not Protected

PROTECTION IS NOT USUALLY REQUIRED when you are dowsing for yourself, but if you are dowsing for anyone other than yourself, it is important that you not take on any of their detrimental energies.

Empathy is overrated and does nothing to help another person. Empathy means you are feeling what they feel, and energetically, that means you are taking on their stuff. People become wounded healers in this way. We applaud sympathy and compassion, but we urge you never to take on other people's stuff. If you are not a trained shaman, you won't help them, and you will hurt yourself.

People who have too much of a tendency to empathy sometimes discover they were shamans in a past life, so when presented with someone who needs healing, they automatically take on that person's energy. However, in this life, if you have not been trained as a shaman, doing that will harm you and not help them.

Any kind of healing activity or dipping into energies can expose you to detrimental forces, so we advise you to use protection when dowsing for anyone other than yourself. There are many good books written on protection, so do some research and use a method that resonates with you.

Protection basically comes from the intention not to take on energies that are detrimental or be affected by them. That intention can be in the form of a simple statement, or you can anchor your intention using a crystal, symbol or by asking for spiritual helpers. Always do protection before working on others, and use dowsing to determine your level of protection on a scale of 0-10. If it isn't 10, don't dowse for that person or animal. Here is a sample dowsing question to test your protection:

On a scale of 0-10, with 10 being totally protected from any noxious or detrimental energies while I dowse, what level of protection do I have at this time?

If it isn't a 10, use a statement with or without an anchor and retest using the same dowsing question. Never dowse if you can't get adequate protection.

∽

Not Enough Training Or Practice

THIS IS COMMON SENSE, but many intelligent people are so eager to do something that they overstep their level of competence. Kids go joy riding in cars and crash, or they play with matches and start a fire by accident. Dowsing is a powerful technique, but it is also a skill, and mastering a skill requires practice and training.

Too often, we see enthusiastic people pick up a pendulum with little training beyond how to get a yes/no answer, just like kids playing with a ouija board, and like a ouija board, dowsing can be risky if you do it without proper training.

Dowsing, as you know, isn't just about getting your pendulum to give a 'yes' or 'no' response. In fact, if you have had training, you realize that a pendulum moving is not proof of dowsing. If you aren't in a dowsing state, your pendulum will still move, but it will give you the answer your brain expects. If you don't know how to ask a good dowsing question, your answer will be meaningless, or at least unreliable.

Try to be patient as you learn dowsing and start with simple, everyday subjects to dowse about. Use topics you are curious about or interested in that will improve your life, like which movie to rent or what book to read or which course to take for your goals. Keep a journal and learn from your mistakes. As you see your accuracy improve, start asking harder questions that challenge your detachment. Be sure to practice letting go of fear through self-work of some kind. You will be able to tell if you are detached or not.

As your accuracy improves, challenge yourself more. Have a dowsing buddy if possible whom you can share your journey with and who can back up your dowsing.

Anyone can learn to be an accurate dowser, but for 99.9% of us, it takes time and effort to master dowsing. We encourage you to use the Resources section to find ways of taking your dowsing to the next level.

For health dowsers it is important to have enough training in human biology and health. How much you need depends on you. Get the training you need to feel you understand human health well enough to ask good questions and interpret the answers. If you don't have adequate grounding in Biology and health, your accuracy will be less than if you have a good foundation in those topics.

Ethical Challenges

WHEN YOU DOWSE FOR YOURSELF, you are always being an ethical dowser. If you dowse about anyone else, you must have their permission before you dowse, because dowsing is like tapping a phone or opening someone's mail to get personal information. You want to be an ethical dowser, and all that takes is choosing never to dowse about another person without their permission.

This can be challenging if you believe you can help a friend or loved one, but they refuse your help. But you must allow them free will, even if you disagree with their choice. You may want your uncle to quit smoking, but it isn't appropriate to go into his house without permission and throw out his cigarettes. He'll just buy more, anyway.

Hardly anyone talks about dowsing ethics, but we think it's a big deal. In fact, we've written a book on the subject. Dowsing is a power, and if you choose to wield any power, you need to think about how to do so ethically.

Karmically, if you ignore other people's boundaries, you create negative karma and invite the same behavior towards yourself. So in a way, being an ethical dowser is a selfish choice, because you don't want anyone trampling on your free will.

11

THE HEALING PROCESS

Introduction

Health dowsing is not a healing method, and this book is not a course in healing. You will need to pursue whatever path feels right to you to help healing take place. You may want to use dowsing to guide you to a good healing team. Or you may want to play a more active role and heal yourself using a method that you dowse will work for your goals.

Either way, it is very useful to have a couple of healing modalities in your tool kit. Each healing method has its own vibration, and none cure everything. Pick one or two methods that resonate with you, learn them and use them. Allow yourself to change over time and drop a method if it no longer serves you, learning a new one as needed.

In this chapter we will discuss the use of dowsing to help you pick the most effective healing method, remedy or energy clearing method for your needs. Obviously, we can't talk about all methods, but you can apply what you learn in this chapter to any healing method. Our goal is to show you that there are a variety of approaches, all of which are valid.

We also discuss the role of health dowsing in helping you maintain optimal health, because we don't want you only to use it when things go wrong. Health dowsing is valuable as a maintenance tool as well.

Healing Modalities

THERE ARE many healing methods you can work with. Healing modalities, except for surgery, tend to be methods that are practiced more than once to achieve your health goals. Natural methods are slower to work in most cases and gentler, with fewer side effects, while surgery and drugs, the main conventional choices, can have many side effects and risks, but if they work, they work faster than natural methods. Whichever path you take, health dowsing can minimize problems and optimize results.

Healing methods come in two forms: those you can do for yourself, and those for which you must hire a professional. It would be a mistake to think that just because a professional charges money, her services are superior to what you can do for yourself. This is only true across the board if you have that belief.

Most people don't have a lot of confidence about their own abilities. They may be interested in Reiki or Jin Shin Jyutsu, and they may wholeheartedly believe in the efficacy of those methods, but only in someone else's hands. If you find yourself feeling this way, don't let it stop you from learning a healing technique. Dive in and do your best to master it. Practice often. Experience is the best way to gain confidence.

However, even if you have mastered two or three healing methods, each one has its own energetic frequency, and the best healing method for you to use in a given situation depends on the frequency of the issue. There is no one method that cures everything for everyone. This is why sometimes, you may well need to go to a professional, because your tools may not be the best match for your goals, but don't let that keep you from learning a healing method or three.

Dowsing is the best way to pick an effective healing method for your unique challenge. Remember to be detached and open to whatever the answer is. Don't push it away because you are afraid it will cost too much. You can decide whether or not to follow through after you get the answer.

Self-healing Modalities

There are too many self-healing modalities to mention in this book. We have become masterful at quite a few ourselves, and we loved all of them. They all worked, but none of them worked on everything. That's why we went on to learn new methods. Learning any method is a journey that will help you grow, so it is never a waste, but do be careful about your investment. Don't invest a lot of time and money into a technique, thinking it will be the cure-all, because there is no such method. Invest in a method you resonate with, that you really want to use, and that you are willing and able to invest in mastering.

Some methods, like Spiritual Response Therapy (SRT) and The Emotion Code, use dowsing in their process and intention for energy transformation. Others use tapping on acupuncture points, as in Emotional Freedom Technique (EFT). Color therapy uses frequencies of colors to heal. Sound healing uses sound frequencies. We have used symbols for healing and energy transformation. In fact, there are an infinite number of healing methods for you to choose from.

We suggest that you let your intuition guide you in choosing what method to learn. You will be attracted to methods that resonate with you. You can use your rational mind to research the method, find out the cost of training and see what applications it has and what people say about it. Then, you can use dowsing to help you decide whether that method is right for your specific goals, or to find the best teacher of that method for your needs and budget.

Here is a sample dowsing question for choosing what method to learn:

On a scale of 0 to 10, with 8 or higher meaning it will be worth my investment and significantly help me reach my stated goals (you can add a period of time, if you wish, such as 'within the next year'), how does _____(name the healing method) rank?

If you get less than an 8, search for another method.

What if, instead of dowsing how helpful overall a method would be for your goals, you want to know how useful it would be for healing a particular condition or symptom? Here are some questions:

Is it possible to cure/resolve/clear the root cause of_____(name the condition/symptom) using _____(name the method)?

On a scale of 0 to 10, with 8 or higher meaning I will achieve significant success or progress on healing the cause of _____(name the symptom/s) within _____(give a period of time), how does _____(name the method) rank?

On a scale of 0 to 10, with 8 or higher meaning it will cure/completely resolve _____(name the condition) within _____(give a period of time), how does _____(name the method) rank?

Sometimes when you set out to learn a healing method, you think it's all about a certain problem you have, but your intuition may have guided you to that method for a different and more important, larger purpose. Maybe it's just to help you see things in new ways, so that you are more open to healing. Or perhaps by learning one method, you will be led to another, and that second one is the one which will solve your problem. Or maybe it is to introduce you to someone who will become very important in your healing journey. It is vital to have goals and be focused on them, but try to remember that the path to success is not always straight and smooth, and whatever happens, it can bring you closer to your goals.

Modalities Practiced By Professionals

There are many reasons why you might have to go to a professional to get help in resolving your health challenge. In many cases, those reasons are based on beliefs you have about not being powerful enough to fix it yourself or needing to spend a lot of money to solve a major or longstanding issue. It is therefore wise to clear faulty beliefs having to do with health. But don't beat yourself up. We all need to consult professionals from time to time, and if that is what dowses best, do it, as long as it is within your budget.

If you don't have a budget for hiring a professional, please look into self-healing methods. They are effective.

If you have determined that you need to consult a professional, you will need a list of modalities that you either use or know are available to you, or you can put them in a chart, if you prefer. Always include 'Other' as a choice on the list or chart. This acknowledges that the right answer may not be on the list/chart.

Start with a question that confirms whether a professional can help you.

Will any of the methods on this list/chart significantly improve/resolve the root cause of _____ (name the condition or symptoms) if I get the number of appointments the practitioner recommends?

If you get a no, then you need a bigger list. Really, you should get 'yes' all the time, because 'Other' is an option on the list, so if you get a 'no', then perhaps a professional is not what you need. If you get a 'yes' response, then ask:

Which of the methods on this list/chart is the most effective for my health goals given my budget and the availability in my locale?

If you are very clear about the words here, this means the method that gives the best results on helping improve your health, but for the least amount of investment of money and time and effort from you. It could be that acupuncture would be most effective, but you'd have to drive 100 miles to get a good practitioner. Or it might be that laser therapy would cure you, but it costs $10,000 to get the number of treatments you'd require, and that's not in your budget. You might also want to add in factors like the talent of the practitioner, her manner with clients, or even integrity about telling you when she can't help you any more. Your question needs to include all your goals, so just use the above as starting points. You can make a list of your goals and insert them in the question by saying 'for my goals' or a simple phrase like that.

What if the best method on the list or chart is only a 5 on a scale of 10? That would mean it isn't worth investing in. So be sure to ask:

On a scale of 0 to 10, with 8 or higher meaning the investment will significantly help me reach my health goals overall, how does _____(the best method from the previous dowsing) rank?

You can combine this question with the previous one by asking if there are any methods on the list that rank 8 or higher overall for your health goals, if you prefer. How you ask your questions is up to you, but be sure you include the salient points for your needs.

If you jump straight to asking for the best method, but you have no goals, you might get a big surprise that isn't a lot of fun. Dowsing only answers the question you ask. Dowsing is not about asking someone else to tell you what to do. You have to be clear on your goal, and then dowsing helps guide you to the best action for that goal. If you don't define your goal clearly, you may go off in a wrong direction. It will still offer learning opportunities, but that's not your prime purpose, is it? So be especially clear as to your goals before asking any of these questions.

Remedies

WHEN WE USE THE TERM 'REMEDIES', we are referring to natural medicines that work on the physical and subtle energy bodies to help healing take place. Remedies are substances that you ingest or apply for a period of time to get best results. Dowsing can help you choose the best remedy for your goals.

Remedies include, but are not limited to, things such as:

- Flower remedies
- Homeopathics
- Essential oils
- Supplements
- Herbs

This list is not complete. You can add any remedy that you want to this list, along with 'Other', and dowse it using a question like the following:

On a scale of +10 to -10, with 0 having no effect and negative numbers having a detrimental overall effect, what is the rating of _____ (name the remedy) for my health goal?

This assumes you have created a clear goal. You can use this question to test each remedy. A +8 or higher means the remedy will be very useful for your goals. The +10 to -10 scale will reflect if a remedy will have a negative effect, and that sometimes is useful information. However, you could also use a 0 to 10 scale.

On a scale of 0 to 10, with 8 or higher meaning the remedy will significantly help me reach my health goals, how does _____ (insert the remedy) rank?

You can also make the question more specific by replacing the phrase 'significantly help me reach my health goals' with something more specific, like 'help me attain my health goals within 30 days when used as directed.'

When you have a number of remedies to choose from, you have to drill down and be more specific about price, lack of side effects and speed of results in order to find the best remedy. At first, you can just test for the ones that will help you significantly, and if you find there are many, become more picky about what you want and make the questions more specific. Include any factor that matters to you.

Remedies can be taken at the same time you are doing a healing method, so it is also wise to test both together to see if either one diminishes the positive effects of the other. For example, if you get a 10 for acupuncture and a 9 for homeopathic, and you have dowsed which homeopathic, then you should check the overall effects of the two combined, if you intend to use them at the same time. Here is a sample question:

On a scale of 0 to 10, with 8 or higher being very effective for achieving my health goals, what is the rating of using acupuncture twice a month and the homeopathic _____(insert remedy), for _____(insert dosage and frequency, such as 30C daily, three pellets) during that time?

If you get lower than an 8 for the two things combined, you should try another combination. You don't want to spend money and time on a combination that won't be excellent for your needs.

You can regard pharmaceuticals as remedies and test them if you wish. This is useful when your doctor is open to hearing your opinion. Some doctors are willing to swap out one drug for another when a patient asks for that. You can also test the efficacy of a drug your doctor is proposing for you, prior to filling the prescription, and ask that he name others that he thinks are equally good, and you dowse the efficacy question above and choose one that is 8 or higher on a 0 to 10 scale.

If you are using this procedure for drugs, be sure to also test side effects of any proposed medicine using the process in the 'Evaluating

Side Effects' section of the 'Dowsing Protocols' chapter. Side effects are a bigger concern with drugs than with natural remedies. If you are using a natural remedy, you would be wise to also dowse for side effects, but for most people, they are rare. Herbs and essential oils are the two on the above list that are most likely to have side effects for some people, but usually they are not life-threatening. You can program yourself to get a low number any time the remedy in question has side effects of a certain intensity, such as 3 or higher on a scale of 10. For more details on programming, see the 'Do You Need A Doctor?' section in the 'Dowsing Protocols' chapter.

Energy Clearing & Transformation

THERE IS some overlap in the concepts we are discussing in this chapter. For example, a healing method is usually an energy transformation process. But a remedy is also transforming energy. Healing modalities can be regarded as therapy methods that address the human body, either physical or subtle energy body. Remedies are substances that are taken to resolve a problem.

In this section, we will address methods of energy clearing and transformation that address the outer world or work on another aspect of the inner person that has an impact on physical or mental health. Space clearing, personal clearing, past life work and working on inherited factors are examples of this type of clearing. This book is not a training on these subjects, but it is wise to consider them when you are trying to improve your health. Here, we will just give you a brief summary of each one, and you can do further research if you wish. Dowsing is an excellent tool for determining how useful each of these will be for a given condition or set of symptoms.

Space Clearing

Your environment has many invisible energies that affect your health, from curses to EMFs, and doing regular space clearing, especially if you use dowsing to identify problems, is an important tool for creating optimal health. We recommend regular space clearing for all homes and businesses. How often will depend on how noxious the energies are. Once a month is good for most businesses, while quarterly is often enough for the average home. More frequent clearings are indicated during times of stress.

A dowsing question for determining the overall effect of environmental energies on your health or health challenge is:

On a +10 to -10 scale, with 0 meaning no effect, what is the overall level in effects of energies in my environment on my health?

Zero means no effect. A negative number means the environmental energies are detrimental. A -8 or worse is serious and should be addressed. If you work, you may want to dowse separately for environmental energies at home and work, as one may be worse than the other.

Alternatively, instead of dowsing the overall effect on your health, you can ask how much environmental energies are contributing to or causing a health problem or symptom.

On a scale of 0 to 10, with 0 being no effect and 10 meaning the total cause, what is the level in effects of environmental energies _____(give location, such as 'at home') in terms of causing or exacerbating_____(name the symptom or condition)?

An 8 or higher indicates you need to get a space clearing as soon as possible.

Please note that you should ask the effects of environmental energies on each resident's and pet's health, as the effects will vary. What is -1 for you might be -9 for your dog. So check for each family member and pet.

Personal Clearing

Your subconscious cannot easily be revealed except through dowsing to find out what it believes, yet it has a major role to play in your health. In addition, your emotions have a huge impact on your health. You may be aware of them, but most people 'stuff' negative emotions, leading to health challenges. Dowsing is useful for identifying subconscious beliefs, emotions and personal energies that can affect health. There are various clearing methods for transforming those energies once they are identified.

Past Life Clearing

As you saw in the allergies section, past lives do have an effect on your current lifetime. When major trauma occurs, your subconscious often makes a judgment and creates a belief that such and such would not have happened if not for thus and so. You can use dowsing to investigate your past lives, but that type of dowsing is called intangible target dowsing, meaning you can't verify the accuracy of results, unless the condition or symptom disappear after clearing, in which case you may assume past lives were the problem.

A dowsing question for determining past life effects on health is:

On a 0 to 10 scale, with 0 being no effect and 10 being the most impact possible, what is the level in effects of past lives on _____(name the condition or symptom)?

An 8 or higher would indicate you might want to look into clearing past lives yourself, as we described in the allergies section of the 'Dowsing Protocols' chapter, or you can seek a professional.

Clearing Inherited Factors

Traumas, programs, epigenetic factors and genetic factors are examples of inherited patterns that can affect your health. When you see health patterns that run in a family, you may be looking at this type of root cause. If dowsing shows that your health issue has inherited factors as a significant cause, you might want to dowse whether a tapping therapy, The Emotion Code or simple intention would be an effective way of clearing those energies and their effects permanently.

∽

Maintaining Health

THE BEST WAY TO be healthy is to stay healthy. You can use health dowsing to help you overcome health problems, but if you only use it for that, you are missing out on a huge benefit of health dowsing. Your intuition, focused through dowsing, will guide you to ways of maintaining and improving your health, so that you always experience optimal health, and this will aid you in optimal longevity.

Even if you are currently working to resolve a health problem, it would be advantageous to implement an ongoing health program, as these things do indeed help resolve illness. Focusing on optimal health almost every day will yield good results, especially if you do it without fear and negativity.

There are some obvious areas you want to work on:

- Get the optimal eating plan for your goals and needs. Be flexible about adapting over time. Measure results.
- Exercise often. Walking is terrific exercise. A rebounder is a good investment. You don't need to join a gym. Get out in Nature and in the sunlight. Move your body.
- Do a practice that harmonizes energy. Tai chi, yoga, chi gong and other methods strengthen the body and allow for good energy flow, aiding health.
- Try meditation or self-hypnosis or visualization and reduce stress. Making time to just 'be' is very valuable for your health and creates balance in a world that emphasizes doing.
- Use a simple balancing and healing method regularly such as toning or color therapy. Toning is particularly easy and costs nothing, but is very powerful.

Doing any of the above focuses your energy on positive outcomes, but don't feel that if you don't do all of the above, your health will suffer. It is very easy to pile responsibilities on yourself and then feel like a failure when you can't find the time to do it all. Start small and do just one thing with focused intention, and add things slowly. Healing is a journey. You start each day with a chance to become healthier and happier, and dowsing will help guide you as you chart your course.

12

GOING BEYOND

Introduction

If health dowsing were only about answering your health questions and helping you achieve your health goals, it would be priceless. This is why we committed to becoming masterful health dowsers years ago. But along the way, we discovered unexpected benefits. These benefits blossomed from the changes we had to make in ourselves in order to become better health dowsers.

Dowsing thus became for us a personal growth process as well. In this chapter, we share some of the ahas that have come to us, so that you may be inspired to do more than just regard health dowsing as a tool for getting answers. By developing your intuition and allowing yourself to use your intuitive senses, you are activating latent human potential that is nothing short of a superpower.

If you skip this section, you can still become a masterful health dowser, and you may even rediscover these 'truths' along the way. But if you have your eyes open to the possibilities, you may experience faster, smoother growth than we did.

Developing Intuition

EVERYONE HAS INTUITIVE SENSES. In most people, they are latent. Some people are more intuitive than others, but in our modern culture, intuition is not valued, because it cannot be measured or controlled. That is, until you learn to dowse.

Dowsing is a way of focusing your intuitive senses. Instead of waiting for an intuitive hit or a hunch, with dowsing, you can give your attention to a particular subject and get information using your intuition. Being able to focus your intuition in this way trains you in the use of your intuitive senses.

If you are using a tool such as a pendulum, you will tend to focus on the tool to the exclusion of all else, because that is natural. This is one reason we encourage you to use deviceless dowsing. If you are blink dowsing or body swaying, you are paying attention to your body movement, but by listening to your body, you are also open to getting other intuitive responses.

Everyone is different, so we can't tell you exactly what to look for. If you are visual, you might get a flash of a vision. If you tend to the auditory, you might hear something. If you are the type who gets gut reactions, you may feel something in some part of your body. The more you dowse, and the more you pay attention to patterns of bodily responses, the sooner you can pair those responses with meaningful information.

Sometimes the information is specific to the question you asked. Instead of getting just a simple 'yes' response, you also get a picture of the answer in context that is much richer and more helpful. An example is when you are dowsing about a past life, it is a slow, stepwise procedure to dowse about it, but as you are dowsing, you can get a complete awareness or picture of that life instantly. If you wonder whether you 'made it up', just dowse the accuracy of the details.

At other times, the information you get is related to technique or something general, such as you get a feeling that you shouldn't be dowsing about something, and later you find out you didn't have protection and the energy was very detrimental. By recognizing that reaction, you save yourself a lot of trouble.

We all have multiple intuitive senses, and some will be dominant or easier for you to access, but practice will improve results in all of them. By using deviceless techniques, you will speed this process considerably. Keeping a journal will help you identify patterns and meanings.

Ideally, wouldn't it be great not to have to dowse to get answers? Too many people regard dowsing as the end point of intuition development, but to us, the real advanced viewpoint is to go beyond dowsing to no longer needing to go through the dowsing process, but to just 'know' what the best path for your goals is. It requires a lot of practice to get to that point; we are still working on it, but it is lots of fun to go beyond dowsing to living intuitively.

New Ways Of Thinking

AS YOU PROGRESS on your path to healing, you will learn the truth of the saying that you can't fix a problem using the same thinking or action that got you there in the first place. One of the problems (in our opinion) with conventional medicine is that it allows you to continue to make poor choices by suppressing the symptoms that are a message that you need to change your ways. Yes, it is nice not to have to change what we do, but if you want to improve your health, it is a must, and the sooner a person acknowledges that, the sooner they can begin to heal.

There are many ways of thinking and doing things that you may have to change or surrender completely in order to reach your health goals, but it will be worth it in the long run. It could be something as simple as giving up junk food, stopping smoking or walking more. Or it could be something harder to measure such as releasing negative beliefs or seeing yourself as a victor instead of a victim. Whether the change is what appears to be a simple outer change or a more complex inner one, it usually requires a level of commitment to accomplish.

Dowsing is very useful for helping you choose the direction that will help shift the energy needed for healing. Try to see this process as an adventure that will help you experience greater health and well-being.

We have found that as we changed our minds, we healed our bodies, our relationships and our finances. It isn't necessarily easy to think in new ways, but the benefits are amazing.

~

Empowerment

IF YOU CHOOSE to become a health dowser, you are choosing to be empowered. You are taking charge of your health and your life experience. This is huge. Most people in our culture entrust their health to someone else, and then, only when they feel they are in danger of losing it.

It is impossible to estimate the value of simply taking charge of some aspect of your life. When you become a health dowser, you are saying you want a certain health experience. Most humans go through life never consciously creating the health they want. You are using health dowsing as a powerful tool for creating health and well-being.

When you become empowered about health, you begin to realize you can choose to be empowered in other ways. You can become financially empowered. You can steer your own career. You can choose relationships that empower you. By becoming a health dowser, you can awaken to the power of choosing. Choosing means focus. Focus means having goals and putting energy into an outcome. These are key steps to manifesting. Health dowsing thus is an effective tool in manifesting what you desire: good health and much more.

Positive Focus

AS THEY SAY in the Law Of Attraction, like attracts like, and what you give attention to, expands. While this statement may or may not make sense to you, the fact remains that in our culture, negative focus is more common than positive. There is a tendency to worry about what will go wrong and to fear what you do not want to experience. The fact is that those tendencies contribute to negative outcomes.

As a health dowser, you have learned to consciously create health goals and to ask questions about how to obtain them. Your focus has turned from fear of ill health to constructing good health. This positive focus will spill over into other areas of your life when you see how successful it is. You will begin to see that the worries, anxieties and fears only contribute to negative results.

Changing your focus from negative to positive is not as easy as flicking a switch. Negative thinking is a pattern that is programmed into most of us. Trauma cements it in place. To focus on what you want instead of what you don't want will require a lot of conscious choices and actions, but don't worry, each time you choose positive focus, you are creating a new pattern that will increase your positive outcomes.

No Longer Be A Victim

AN ENERGY that goes along with disempowerment is victimhood. Both energies are rampant in all human societies. There is nothing harder to control than someone who knows their own mind and has self-confidence. That may be one reason that there is so much subtle and direct programming of humans by religion and governments to convince them they need someone else to do their thinking for them, that they are not good enough or smart enough or powerful enough to do anything on their own, and that they must be victims.

The energy of being a victim is contradictory to being a health dowser. If you choose to dowse for your health, you are stepping into your power, accepting that you can take action to create better health for yourself. This attitude will not only benefit your health, it will likely spread into other areas of your life, waking you up to your full potential as a human being.

Here are some examples of subtle and not-so-subtle ways you are programmed to be a victim of poor health and unable to do anything about changing it yourself:

- You are told that your genes determine your health, which makes you a victim of them. This has been proven wrong, but people are being urged to get genetic testing and take drastic actions based on results, as if genes always express one way. This is false.
- Many people find that their doctor won't listen to their opinion and makes them feel unable to participate in their health care process because they didn't go to medical school. They tell you what to do, and if you have questions, you are belittled or in some cases shown the door. This attitude is not universal, but it is prevalent enough that many patients feel like helpless victims of the health care system.
- The media points out all the ways our planet is being poisoned, and by extension, how you are being poisoned,

by toxins in air, water and food. Often, it gets to the point that you feel you cannot avoid damage to your health, because you can't stop radiation leaks that are poisoning the ocean. You can't stop the spraying in the skies with toxic substances. You can't stop industry from dumping toxins in the earth that poison water sources. This makes you feel that you cannot control factors that affect your health.

- You may be horrified by what the pharmaceutical companies are doing to force people to use their products, when they are well aware of the dangers and side effects. When laws make corporations not answerable for practices that harm people's health, and when corporations manage to get laws passed to force people to use their products, it is easy to feel you are a victim to corporate greed.

Being a victim is not compatible with being a health dowser. While the above situations exist, and they can be very distressing to think about, it is important to focus on taking action that you believe will make your life healthier. Do not focus on things over which you have no control. Take control of the things you can.

Your thoughts are the most important factor in your health, so do whatever it takes to shift yourself into victor mode whenever you find yourself feeling like a victim. Perception becomes reality. You will be amazed at how much your life improves overall if you practice being a victor instead of a victim.

Being Unconventional

IF YOU HAVE CHOSEN to be a health dowser, you are definitely not a conventional thinker. But for a time, you can put health dowsing in a separate box from the rest of your life and assure yourself that you are still a 'normal' person. This will especially be true for people who are concerned about being rejected or judged if they do not conform.

You have a right to make this choice, but if you use health dowsing to the fullest extent, it is inevitable that someone will find out. You will need to tell your doctor, or you will have to tell your spouse.

Being unconventional is not a bad thing. Of course, we all want to be loved for who we are, and unconditional love is rare, so we tend to hide things we fear will lead to rejection or shaming by those closest to us.

Becoming a dowser of any kind often leads to conflict with those closest to you. Some people have religious prejudices that make them feel dowsing is a tool of the devil. Others think of it as a New Age trick, and if you are a dowser, you are an airhead at the very least and a charlatan at the worst. Other people might simply become uncomfortable if they know you dowse, and not even understand why.

The main reason you might be pressured into conventional behavior is that people are afraid of what they don't understand. They are even more afraid of people showing they have a mind of their own and are willing to accept and use power. This makes sense when you understand that fear, victimhood and powerlessness are the most common energies people resonate with, and if you stray too far from those energies, you won't be a 'match' with other people. The difference in energetic frequency will manifest as negative behavior towards you and pressure to get you back in line. It can lead to broken relationships, as people tend to associate mainly with people who resonate with similar energy.

This can be frightening, especially to those who prefer to have a 'tribe' to support them. As a health dowser, you may find you need to gather a whole new tribe of people to interact with. You can frequent dowsing conventions, chapter meetings and online groups. The latter is in fact how we met back in 2000, when we were stepping away from conventional reality as we became serious dowsers. Don't feel forced to be what others want you to be. Choose what you want to be and find others who respect your choice. It is always possible to find your tribe if you have the courage to look for them and leave behind relationships that no longer are supportive.

∼

What If Not All Dis-ease Is Physical?

OFTEN, when you start out as a health dowser, you are focused on physical symptoms and physical solutions, like supplements, therapies and dietary changes. If you continue to practice health dowsing, and if you keep an open mind and learn more about health, you may find yourself looking at dis-ease in a whole new way, and that perspective will be quite empowering.

You may start by believing that stress and emotions have a strong effect on your physical health. In fact, most conventional doctors agree with this, though they tend not to dwell on it, because they don't have many tools in their toolbox to help you with those problems. (Plus it won't make them any money.)

As a health dowser, you can learn techniques for reducing stress and releasing negative emotions, and you will see positive changes in your health as a result. You can also dive into the subject of vibrational healing, the subtle energy body and the real causes of physical dis-ease. You may find yourself drawn to the Law Of Attraction, because it explains so much about why health problems occur and how you can get yourself back on track to experiencing the health you want.

Health goes way beyond the physical. You are not just a physical machine like a car that needs gas and oil and regular maintenance to run smoothly. You are not even a complicated physical machine like a computer, that works only as well as its hardware and software allow it to. You are a spiritual being having a physical experience in the human body, and there are many energetic, invisible factors affecting your health, and the more you know about them, the more empowered you become to experience wellness.

We hope that health dowsing not only becomes a valuable tool for you to create better health, but that you allow it to lead you to see the world in whole new ways that will attract well-being into all areas of your life, from your relationships, to finances to your career, because that is what it did for us, and we think it could do the same for you.

13

BONUS: QUESTIONS FROM "ASK THE RIGHT QUESTION"

This material is lifted from the health dowsing chapter in our book *Ask The Right Question: The Essential Sourcebook Of Good Dowsing Questions*. It has not been altered, and there will be repetition with the other content in this book, but we wanted to give you this as a bonus. Health dowsing is just one section of *Ask The Right Question*, and if you like this chapter, we urge you to pick up a copy of the book.

∽

Using The Questions In This Bonus Section

THIS CHAPTER IS DIVIDED into a number of subjects that we have found are of common interest to dowsers. Questions will be listed along with the goals you have for asking them. For those who want to create their own question, notes are added that will give you tips on how to customize dowsing questions on that subject. There will be some repetition, because this material is lifted from another book. We have not altered the content in any way.

∽

Overall Health

A good place to start when health dowsing is to get an overall picture of how your physical body is doing; where it is strong and where it could use some assistance to become stronger. You can dowse the answers to whichever questions you want, and then look at the results to get a picture of your overall physical health.

On a scale of +10 to -10, with 0 being average for my gender, age and culture, what is my overall physical health at this time?

Obviously, a 0 is average; minus numbers are less than average; plus numbers are better than average.

System Health

You can test the physical health of various organs and systems using the same type of question by substituting the following one by one in the blank:

(You may look these up online to get more complete definitions)

Nervous System: central nervous system (brain) and nerves

Circulatory System: heart, arteries, veins

Reproductive System: ovaries, uterus, testes

Endocrine System: glands like thyroid, adrenals, pancreas

Digestive System: stomach, intestines, mouth

Urinary System: bladder

Skeletal System: bones, ligaments, tendons, cartilage

Respiratory System: lungs

Muscle System: muscles, sometimes includes the heart

Integumentary System: hair, skin, nails

Lymphatic system

On a scale of +10 to -10, with 0 being average for my gender, age and culture, what is the overall physical health of my _____ System at this time?

Write the answers down and get a picture of how your overall health is doing in each area.

Organ Health

You can then dig deeper and see which part of a particular system is weakest. Using a search engine or book, list the organs and parts of each system. Let's use the Digestive System as an example:

The parts of the Digestive System are:

- salivary glands
- esophagus
- stomach
- liver
- gall bladder
- pancreas
- intestines
- rectum
- anus

Let's say you got a lower number than you would like for the physical health of your digestive system. Your next step is to find out where you need to focus your effort in healing and balancing it.

So you ask the same question again, this time substituting, one at a time, the different parts of the digestive system. Write the answers down.

On a scale of +10 to -10, with 0 being average for my gender, age and culture, what is the overall physical health of my _____ at this time?

When To Take Action On The Above

In general, we would regard -8 or worse to be a number that would cause us to want to take action right away to balance and heal the system (if we found that another dowser agreed with our answers, or a doctor's test agreed). If you are in the low minus numbers, you can take gentle action. You can even work to improve your rating if you got above 0. Obviously, an 8 or above is a terrific place to be.

Check out Dowsing Supplements, Remedies and Therapies and When To Consult a Professional if you need to do some work on some part of your body.

Key Subjects To Test

There are some processes or situations that can affect health that don't always reside in a single system or organ, yet they can contribute to or indicate a major health imbalance. These aspects are:

- toxicity
- inflammation
- infection
- trauma
- cancer energy
- parasites

Test for each subject by substituting one by one in the question below, and write your answers down.

On a scale of 0 to 10, with 0 being none and 10 being the worst/most it could be, what is the level/degree of physical_____ in my physical body at this time?

The reason we ask about 'physical' toxicity, inflammation, etc. Is that you can have energetic issues, and they require different treatment. So you can test the level of energetic toxicity, inflammation, etc. separately.

Interpreting Results On The Previous Question

We have found that 0-3 is fairly common for most of the subjects in the previous question, though 0 is of course the best answer to get. At 3, one tends to start seeing physical symptoms. At 8, whatever is causing the problem really needs attention, usually by a professional.

∽

Aura

It will be useful to take a course or at least read a good book about the aura to understand it better. Barbara Brennan's book *Hands of Light* is very helpful in this regard. However, it is also very detailed, and so this chapter will present a much more abbreviated version of dowsing the health of the aura which will allow even beginners to use dowsing to check the health of their auras. Those who want to dive deeper should get Barbara's book.

The aura has layers. The seven layers operate on different planes, with three of them on the physical plane. You can have problems at any level, and the problems can be many different types. However, for the purposes of this book, we won't get into which layer is affected, but instead will do an overall evaluation to find problems and resolve them.

What is the overall health of my aura at this time, on a scale of 0 to 10, with 10 being optimal health for me?

An 8 or above is considered a very good score. Lower means that there is probably something going on that is affecting the integrity of the aura. Using a book or other resource, make a list of the potential problems you can have with your aura. Examples could be:

- tear
- burn
- infection
- block

You can substitute mechanisms into the following question one by one to find out what the problem is (and remember there may be more than one):

Are there any _____ at this time in my aura that are having a significant effect on the health and well-being of my aura?

If you get yes, you can then go to remedies/therapies and find out what will help resolve the issue.

~

Chakras

Your body has many minor chakras, but 7 major ones. Problems with the chakras can lead to physical ailments. *Hands of Light* is a very good book that covers dowsing the chakras in detail. We won't go into that depth here. Instead, this is a good starting point for evaluating your chakra function using dowsing.

There are two obvious ways to dowse your chakras. Maggie was introduced to dowsing through her Karuna Reiki Master Teacher class, where the instructor pulled out a pendulum and showed that the movement of the pendulum, when held over the chakras, gave information about how that chakra was functioning. In Barbara Brennan's book, she details the types of pendulum movements. So if you are interested in taking it further, definitely refer to her book.

For the purposes of this book, we will simplify the process so you can begin to get useful information about the functioning of the chakras. There are a few basic pendulum movements you will see when you evaluate the chakra:

1) Circular (in either direction)

2) Linear (in various directions/angles)

3) No movement at all

4) A complex daisy-like series of 'flower petal' circles (in either direction)

If you are evaluating someone else's chakras, you can have them lie on their back while you hold the pendulum over each chakra, asking to see the function. If you are evaluating your own chakras or working long distance with someone, you can just ask to see the function of whatever chakra. In either case, you start the pendulum in a neutral swing or circle, then ask to see how that chakra is working.

Be patient and allow the pendulum to settle into whatever movement is appropriate. It may even need to reverse direction, so make sure you give it a good swing to start, so it has plenty of motion to work with.

Here is a very simplified summary of what the different pendulum motions mean:

1) Circular: normal, size of circle showing how much energy flowing or how open

2) Linear: lines indicate there is some kind of block to normal function

3) No movement means the chakra is shut down

4) A daisy shape indicates a lot of transformational energy is present

A nice, big circle is usually a 'good' thing. The daisy shape shows a person is changing, which is neither good nor bad, but depends on various factors. Linear usually means some work would be advisable. A shut down chakra can lead to illness, pain and other negative consequences, so it is wise to address it immediately.

You can use dowsing to get further information about causes of problems and to choose the best way to remedy dysfunction.

Bioelectromagnetic Field

Your body's electromagnetic field, which relates to the activity of your brain and heart, has a huge but little-known impact on your health, well-being and ability to manifest your desires. Dowsing is an excellent tool for evaluating your EM Field; the causes of problems; and how to strengthen it.

Michele Fitzgerald of the Senzar Learning Center is the one who pioneered the work on the EM Field and how it relates to various aspects of your life back in 2009. It is beyond the scope of this book to go into full detail about the EM Field, so if you want to dive deeper into this important subject, you will want to consult the Resources section for a link to Michele's website.

Note: The EM Field is not your aura, nor does it have anything to do with EMFs (electromagnetic fields). It is generated by the activity of the brain and heart, and it is electromagnetic in origin. A stronger EM Field gives you greater protection of all kinds and helps you manifest positive outcomes more easily. You feel good and have a higher energy level when your EM Field is strong.

Sadly, our research shows that most people have an EM Field operating at less than 35%. In most cases, much less. You don't have to be a dowser to know when your EM Field is low. You feel exhausted and unmotivated and struggle to just do what needs doing.

The EM Field is actually rather easy to bring into the 30% range in most cases, and that will give you a real boost of energy and motivation. We have found color therapy seems to work well on most people for strengthening a weak EM Field.

Evaluate Your EM Field

On a scale of 0 to 100%, with 100% being the best and most optimal functioning, what is the value of my EM Field as an average over the last 7 days?

Note that you can dowse several times for several different time periods to get a feel for how your EM Field has been operating over time. Instead of the 7 day average, you can test the 30 day/60 day/1 year averages.

Generally we test a 7 day average, because even thinking about testing it and wanting it to be a higher value will actually raise the level temporarily. The EM Field value varies over a +10% to -10% range over the course of a given day. So if you got 30% (which most people won't), then your EM Field probably has been between 20-40% over that time period.

Causes Of EM Field Issues

There are actually many variables that can cause your EM Field to crash or be very low. Some have to do with poor boundaries and beliefs allowing others' energies to affect you. Some have to do with external electromagnetic fields we all are exposed to, like wifi and other EMFs. If you are interested in learning more about the EM Field and what can affect it, check into Michele Fitzgerald's trainings through the link in the Resources section.

Repairing The EM Field

Most people will find they are below 30% when they dowse their EM Field value. We have found color therapy to be the easiest way to repair the EM Field. The most common colors that dowse as appropriate are: red, blue, purple, silver and gold.

Dowse which color or colors are best to help repair, restore and strengthen your EM Field, if it is below 35%.

Is red/blue/purple/silver/gold the best color for me to use to repair, restore and strengthen my EM Field at this time? (Dowse about each color individually.)

Sometimes two colors do better than one. So after you get the first color, ask:

Is using two colors better than using one for me to repair, restore and strengthen my EM Field at this time?

If you get 'yes', then test and find which color is the second color you need to use.

Once you have the color(s) you need, then wear it, look at it or carry it with intention. When wearing it, that means wear that color clothing (it doesn't have to be a large item or on the surface; you can carry a scrap of material that color or wear socks that color). To look at it, choose an item in your environment that is the right color and stare at the color for 60-90 seconds twice a day with intention. To carry the color, use a crayon or colored pencil to color a piece of paper, and put it in your pocket or shoe, wearing it with intention.

Here is the intention to use:

"Please repair, restore and strengthen my EM Field to its highest appropriate level at this time."

How long do you do this? Do it until your EM Field tests at least in the 30s and you feel much better. How long will that take? In most cases, less than two weeks. Sometimes one or two days.

If you are unable to get your field at least into the 30s by doing color therapy, you probably have an unusual mechanism affecting you, and you could benefit from getting professional help to discover the cause and resolve it. We suggest you take Michele's course if this happens, because there are very few professionals aware of the EM Field and how to repair it

Supplements

Dowsing for supplements is perhaps one of the most common practical applications of dowsing. Yet most people do not dowse their supplements in such a way that they reap the most benefits they can. In this section, we will help show you how you can use dowsing to evaluate supplements, side effects, how long it will take to see results and how your entire supplement program is working for you. We'll also give you some valuable tips on supplement dowsing that will save you a lot of money and give you better results.

Remember that supplements work slowly. It can take up to 120 days for them to give results, unless your system is really deficient, in which case you may see quick results. So when you find something, give it a fair chance to work.

Note: You can use all these same questions to test the usefulness of herbal and homeopathic remedies, flower essences and essential oils for helping you achieve goals with symptoms and conditions.

Is A Supplement Or Remedy What You Need?

There's a lot of controversy, and always has been, about supplements and their usefulness. In a sense everyone is correct. Supplements are useless if they are poor quality. Don't waste money on cheap supplements. Supplements are NOT a substitute for a good diet. Research and find the best, healthiest diet you can, and you won't need as many supplements.

Your body is changing constantly, and its need for various minerals and vitamins changes over time. So any single supplement or program probably is not going to be the lifetime solution for you. And finally, good supplements are expensive, but you take supplements to achieve excellent health. If they work, you won't be sick; you won't have degenerative disease; you'll live a more active, healthy life. What's that worth to you?

For general supplementation, as in creating a balance of minerals and vitamins for optimal physical function, use the following question while testing bottles on a shelf in the health food store, or the products in a catalog or on a website:

Will supplementation by any of these products be an 8 or higher on a scale of 10 (with 10 being the most helpful) for creating excellent immune balance, good energy levels and excellent physical function for my body at this time when taken as directed?

If you get 'no', then it's probably not worth supplementing at this time. If you get 'yes', then you need to find which one or ones to buy. Think about your key requirements and needs for a 'yes' answer: price, side effects, allergic reaction, digestibility, absorbability, how quickly they act, how effective they are, etc. Everyone has different requirements, so put all yours together and say a 10 is a product that fulfills all of them to your satisfaction.

Next, be very clear about why you want to take supplements. What is excellent health to you? High energy levels? Good digestion? Feeling pain free? Staying healthy instead of catching colds? Etc. Don't expect to get a good answer if you are unclear about how you define health.

Are any of these products an 8 or higher on a scale of 10 for reaching my overall health goals at this time when taken as directed?

If you get a lot of possible products, trim the list down by asking if any are a 10 on a scale of 10, then dowse among them. If you don't get any that are 8 or better, go to another website, store or provider and test their products. Don't waste money on anything that is less than an 8 as a rule.

Ideally you want to get down to one product that is a 10 and then give it a try. If you are particularly deficient, this may not be possible. If you have a large overall deficiency, our advice is to get on an excellent combination vitamin/mineral supplement instead of treating symptoms. Most of your symptoms will often disappear if you balance your system with a good overall supplement that covers all the bases. Then you can address any lingering issues, which should be far fewer. Give the plan 90-120 days to work. Remember to see a doctor if your symptoms are serious.

Factors To Consider When Dowsing Supplements And Remedies

Your digestion is a huge factor in the effectiveness of your supplements. You must absorb something for it to work. If your digestive system is inflamed or you have food allergies or leaky gut, you may not get the results promised. If you know you have a digestive challenge, spend time healing your gut. There are many natural ways to do this, and it is worth the effort.

Supplementation ideally should be a short term phenomenon. By short term, we mean not your whole life. It is best to get your nutrients from your diet. However, even a good organic diet with lots of fruits and veggies often won't provide enough minerals, due to the sorely depleted state of soils. Minerals are critical for bodily function, and your dowsing will help you determine when you need additional ones.

Anything can be an allergen. Even something 'good'. Be sure to test for whether you have any allergic or sensitivity reaction to a given supplement or any ingredient in it (there are a shocking number of 'extra' ingredients) before buying it. See the later section on this topic.

It's generally unwise to supplement only one mineral, like calcium. That's because so many minerals work in conjunction with others, and when you raise the value of one, you may inadvertently create an imbalance with another. Magnesium, for example, is closely tied to calcium. Potassium depends on magnesium. And so on. You want an optimal balance in your body of all minerals. So unless you have been diagnosed with a mineral deficiency, don't load one mineral, or you may just create another deficiency.

It's best to work with a health care professional to determine the best overall strategy of supplementation for your needs. If that professional wants to recommend their own brand of product, you can then elect to dowse and see if their suggestion is an 8 or better for your goals.

How Long To Take It?

Be patient about results. But don't think you'll need to supplement forever. You can dowse what the optimal time length to take the chosen supplement will be.

How long would it be best for me to take this supplement to reach my health goals:

More than 30 days?

More than 60 days?

More than 90 days?

Just change the question until you get the time frame that says 'yes'. An alternative question that is just as good, once you pick a particular supplement, would be:

How many bottles of this supplement taken at the suggested dosage will be required for me to reach my health goals?

1?

2?

3?

If you are not happy with how large the numbers/time get, then feel free to check and see if another product from another store or catalog can do better overall for you.

Evaluating Results

Assuming you marked the calendar for how long it would take to get results, when that date arrives, you want to evaluate your results. This means ask yourself how much, if any, things have improved. Do you have more energy? Are you sleeping better? Or whatever your goals were.

If results can't be gotten by tuning in to your body, then dowse as needed to gauge the success. For example, if you did a round of digestive supplements to help you absorb your food better, you may not be sure if they are working, because you didn't have obvious symptoms. In cases like that, you can dowse your progress by testing the original question about your digestion and see if the results have improved. Hopefully you wrote the first answer down and dated it. That's why the charts at the end of each chapter have columns.

How Good Is Your Whole Supplement Program?

A mistake often made, even by professionals, is to only test a single supplement for effectiveness. But if you are taking any other supplements, it is important to test how adding that new supplement into your entire program is going to affect the overall performance of the program.

While the supplement may test as being very helpful for the particular symptom you have, its effectiveness may go down when combined with other supplements. Indeed, it could lower the effectiveness of other elements of your program. So after finding the best supplement, test the overall effectiveness of your entire supplement program when you add the new supplement to it. As long as it stays 8 or higher, you're fine.

What is the overall effectiveness of my entire program of supplements for my health goals at this time if I include this new product?

If the number has dropped below 8 on a scale of 10, you need to find another supplement to resolve the problem.

Why You Need To Dowse Your Supplements Regularly

Your body is constantly changing. Some days you need more help than others. As your health improves (we are assuming it will, since that is your goal), you will find that you can drop some items from your program. During times of increased stress, you will want to be open to adding some things temporarily. **Always check with your doctor before removing any prescription medication or changing dosages, as some require special programs for withdrawal.**

We suggest that about once a month, you test each individual supplement or remedy and drop any that are under 8 on a scale of 10. Put them aside, as you may need to add them back in later. Then, test the entire program and make sure it's still at least an 8. The idea is to create a program of supplements that have maximum impact on improving your health and immune strength while not taking any that are a waste of time or money.

It's true that anything you put into your body requires energy to be processed. So if you are taking supplements you don't need, you are making unnecessary work for your body. You don't want to do that.

IDENTIFYING Allergies With Dowsing

You can be allergic or sensitive to substances that you ingest, breathe or contact. Often, if you are allergic to one item, you have allergies to others. Allergies and sensitivities feel very much alike in most cases, so we won't distinguish between them for the purpose of dowsing.

There are lists of common allergens online, and you can download one for evaluating yourself. You may have a suspicion or believe you are allergic to something, but put that from your mind and be detached while dowsing about it.

Scales are useful when evaluating allergies, because you will want to deal with allergens that have the most effect on you. We like to use a scale of 0-10 to show the intensity of allergic/sensitive response, with 0 being none and 10 being the most you could show.

For each item you want to test, ask:

How allergic/sensitive am I to _____ on a scale of 0 to 10, with 0 being not allergic at all and 10 being the most allergic I could be?

Make a note of which items you get 8 or higher for, if any. Those are the ones that you want to deal with first. Symptoms often begin to show at 3 or higher.

What Can You Do If You Have Allergies?

There are many paths you can take. Eliminating the allergen from your diet/environment is the first thing we would suggest.

Seek professional help for allergies that are serious or life-threatening, or if they prevent you from living a normal life.

Work on healing your liver, as often you will see an overloaded liver if there are a lot of allergies.

Challenges In Allergy Testing

It isn't always that straightforward to identify an allergen. For example, you may dowse as sensitive to melons, and you may react negatively when you eat them. But is it the melon itself, or is it the molds that are common in melons? Maggie was told by her doctor many years ago that it was just too difficult to track the causes of her allergies down, and he'd just write her a prescription for Seldane. This was unacceptable to her, so she went on to study and heal herself with the help of a variety of holistic practitioners and therapies, including dowsing.

If you find you are sensitive to a lot of fruits and veggies, maybe you are allergic to pesticide residues rather than the fruits and veggies themselves. Switching to organic will help you see which is the problem.

Not all ingredients are listed clearly in many processed foods. For example, garlic is a common allergen that is not always listed as an ingredient when present.

Other common examples of incomplete labeling include wheat gluten, which may be listed as 'vegetable starch', and paprika which may be listed as 'spice'.

We have found that people can actually be allergic to emotions and concepts. For example, you could be allergic to joy, success or financial wealth. If you find you have this type of an allergy, you can clear it the same way you do physical ones. The symptoms you get from allergies to concepts usually won't be physical.

Resolving The Energetic Causes Of Allergies

There are many fine methods for clearing allergies. Ones you can do yourself, if trained, include: EFT (Emotional Freedom Technique) and SRT (Spiritual Response Therapy). Or you could seek professional help of some kind.

If you are not trained in the above, and you don't want to seek professional help, we have found that dowsing about past lives that contributed to the allergic reaction and then clearing those lives is a good way to go, and it will often reduce or remove the allergic response. Since this guide is not about healing methods, we won't go into detail about that here. You can, however, see some details about dowsing past lives in a later section of *Ask The Right Question*.

EVALUATING **Your Diet**

The best diet is actually just a good eating style you can live with that will meet all your nutritional needs. Going on a diet to lose weight rarely works as a permanent solution for being fit and healthy. Instead, we suggest you find a way of eating that you can enjoy and stick with that gives you good health and fitness.

There is no one size fits all diet or lifestyle. For most people, a diet that is organic, non-GMO and has the fewest number of additives will be a good place to start.

Obviously, reducing or eliminating junk food, sugar, sodas and processed food is a good first step. Just doing that will cause you to lose weight and feel more energy. We have had excellent results with eliminating grains from our diet.

Do your due diligence about any particular eating plan or diet, then dowse its effectiveness for your goals.

Make a list of the goals you have for being on this diet, then dowse:

How effective on a scale of 0-10 would the _____ diet be for achieving my health and fitness goals at this time?

An 8 or higher indicates something worth implementing. Or another way of asking it:

What would be the overall Level in Effects of my following the _____ diet on my health and fitness goals on a scale of +10 to -10?

A negative number would mean that the diet would actually drive you backwards along the path toward your goals.

How Long To Diet?

Remember that you are constantly changing. Your body may love a particular diet now, but in a month, it may want a change. Check the value of your diet once a month. If it drops below an 8, perhaps you need to supplement something, or else find a new diet.

You can also dowse how long it will take to achieve your goals with this diet, for example, if you want to lose 10 pounds. Use a question like this:

How long will I need to be on the _____ diet to achieve my goal of losing ten pounds? More than one month? More than two? Etc.

Is One Diet Better Than Others?

You are an individual, and your body knows what it needs. What works for one person may or may not work for you. Dowsing will help you evaluate what diet is worth implementing.

You are always better off with a well-rounded diet that includes all the basic things you need for proper nutrition. Don't follow the food pyramid put out by the government. That's a joke. People are discovering that grains are not a requirement, and in fact they are poor nutritionally and lead to a lot of symptoms. Good quality oils are essential. Organic and non-GMO foods are safest. Pastured, wild-caught and grass-fed meats are best nutritionally and ethically.

If your food is raised in a natural and humane manner, it will be more healthy for you. For example, stressed chickens don't make healthy eggs.

Vegetarian diets have been shown to lead to certain vitamin deficiencies, because a more natural human diet does include animal protein, and vegetables cannot mimic those exactly. If you choose a vegetarian diet, be sure to supplement to make up for that.

We feel that it is best not to regard dietary choice as a moral issue. That type of judgment seems to go along with certain dietary restrictions from ancient religions. As if eating meat on Friday is a sin, or mixing dairy with meat is morally wrong and leads to punishment. We are not making fun of religious dietary restrictions; we just caution you not to use them as a way of feeling superior. A vegetarian diet doesn't make you more spiritual than a meat-eater. If only it were that simple! Getting your foods from sustainable, humane and non-GMO sources shows what you care about. But try not to regard such choices as making you superior to those who do not agree with you.

Evaluating Your Fitness Regime

You can use dowsing to evaluate the effectiveness of a particular fitness regime or type of exercise for you. Write down what your fitness goals are. Then dowse the various options you have, like Pilates, yoga, running, cardio, etc.

What is the overall level in effects for me of participating in _____ as a means of reaching my fitness goals on a scale of +10 to -10, with 0 having no effect and positive numbers having increasingly positive effects?

How long would I need to participate in _____ to reach my stated fitness goals? More than one month? More than two? Etc.

Which Type Of Exercise Is Best For You?

There is no one-size-fits-all fitness regimen. Some people respond better to vigorous workouts, while others find that stressful and respond better to gentle programs like yoga. You can use dowsing to find out what will best suit you if you aren't sure.

Make a list of the types of exercise regimens you are considering. Then dowse each:

On a scale of +10 to -10, with 0 being neutral and positive numbers meaning I would enjoy success and negative numbers meaning I would dislike it/not get results, what is the value of participating in _____ for me at this time for my fitness goals and enjoyment?

∼

Factors To Consider When Dowsing Therapies

You can dowse the effectiveness of a therapy for your goal. You can dowse one that you were inspired about, or you can dowse the one recommended by your health care professional. There are no one-size-fits-all therapies. That is why dowsing is so helpful. You can use dowsing to find out how effective it will be for you, your loved one or your pet.

Therapies sometimes have side effects, especially if they are allopathic in origin. You can use dowsing to determine the level of side effects, or just wrap that into the question when comparing possible therapies. It doesn't matter how good the therapy is for resolving your issue if it just creates other issues.

Sometimes it works out best to use more than one therapy. Sometimes you will see the best results if you do one therapy, then switch to another after a period of time. Dowsing will help you figure out which ones and when to use them.

Which Therapy Is Best?

Make a list of the therapies you want to consider. For example, when treating cancer, your doctor may tell you that you have an option of radiation, chemotherapy, medication, surgery, macrobiotic diet, and several other things.

Write down your goal. Be sure your goal is related to restoring balance and health, not just about getting rid of symptoms. Your goal is to be healthy, feel good and be able to function physically at a very high level. You want to pick the therapy that will get you closest to that goal.

You want to be detached about the results. Don't even bother dowsing if you are fearful or want to get a particular answer. You won't be accurate. In cases like that, you can blind dowse to avoid your emotional reaction if you don't have someone who can dowse for you who isn't attached to results.

Considering all my goals and desiring a minimum of negative side effects, what is the overall level in effects of using _____ (fill in the blank with a therapy) on a scale of +10 to -10 at this time as directed for my specific health goals (as listed), with a positive number meaning it will enhance health, 0 means neutral/no effect and a negative number meaning it will detract from health.

How Long To Use It?

Every person is unique, so how long to use a therapy for best results will depend on the individual. While you probably won't be able to convince your doctor to do radiation or chemotherapy for the amount of time you dowse is best, you will find it useful to dowse how long to take a particular herb or homeopathic for best results.

Considering my specific health goals, what is the best length of time for me to use this therapy to restore balance and health and resolve the cause of my physical symptoms? More than one week? More than one month? Etc.

When you reach the length of time you have dowsed, you can retest to make sure it's still appropriate to quit the therapy. Then you can ask if there is another remedy or therapy that would be an 8 or higher on a scale of 10 for continuing the healing process.

Evaluating Results

You don't always have to dowse to evaluate your results. In most cases, if you have picked an effective therapy or remedy, you will see a reduction in symptoms or a resolution of your problem. But sometimes you can't see or feel the change, so in that case, you can dowse efficacy before you start the therapy and then again after you have done it for the proper amount of time.

For example, if you dowsed that your digestive system had a level of inflammation that was a 7 out of 10, then you did a herbal anti-inflammatory and changed your diet for 30 days, you could retest the level of inflammation in your digestive system at the end of that time and see the change.

If the results still give you a number that shows there is an imbalance, you can work with your health care professional, or if you are a competent health dowser, you can dowse what to do next to continue the healing process.

∼

Do You Need Professional Help?

One of the most useful applications for health dowsing is to help you decide when it is appropriate to invest time and money in professional health care services for you, a loved one or a beloved pet. Even if you have excellent health insurance, it is costly in terms of time to consult with a professional. And for veterinarian consultations and for those who lack insurance, knowing when to go to a doctor guarantees you don't waste money.

We routinely dowse to see if taking our pet to the vet is the most effective way to resolve a physical symptom. Our pets are quite healthy for the most part, and we can go a couple of years without needing to see a vet even though we have 10 pets. In 2013, though, we had a few cases of accidents that caused us concern about 3 of our cats, and in each case, dowsing indicated going to the vet was unnecessary.

Knowing how much it costs to go to the vet, we certainly saved upwards of $1000 or more in vet bills that year through dowsing. And each of the 3 cats recovered very nicely without complications using simple methods available to us at home.

Although this is one of the most useful health dowsing applications, it is not wise to wait until you have a sick pet or child to dowse this question. Practice your dowsing all the time. Learn detachment. Check your answers. Gain confidence in your accuracy. Then when the time comes to dowse this subject, you will be able to get good answers.

Always have a good dowser back up your answers by dowsing for you. Get a second and third opinion and make sure you feel that the answers are accurate. **If in doubt, go to the doctor. Do not play games with the health of yourself or a loved one. Only good health dowsers should attempt to dowse this subject.**

Factors That Affect Your Decision

You probably never thought of it this way, but every time you or someone in your family is ill or has an accident, you make a conscious decision about whether to seek professional help. Sometimes that answer is obvious. You may have an allergy, or your child has the sniffles. You choose to use an over-the-counter remedy and your own knowledge of how to boost the immune system or reduce symptoms instead of going to the doctor, and everything goes well.

On another occasion, your child may fall from her bike, landing on her outstretched hand. The pain is obviously very bad, and the arm is swelling at an alarming rate. You rush her to the emergency room, because you are quite certain the arm or wrist is broken, and it is.

In both of those cases, you decided without dowsing whether it was appropriate to seek outside professional help. But what about the in-between cases? We've all had them happen from time to time.

My experience has been that people in such cases will follow their own judgment. Some will choose to err on the side of being overly cautious, because they wouldn't want to make a mistake and appear to be a bad parent. Others might take the opposite tack and refuse to seek help due to a sense of machismo, not wanting to appear weak, or maybe because they don't feel they should spend money on themselves. Whenever you make decisions based on reasons like these, it's easier for mistakes to happen.

Before you dowse about whether to seek outside help, make a list of factors that you would include in your decision. Not everyone has the same list, and that means that not everyone will get the same answer when they ask the question. Your answer will only be as accurate as the list you have made, so take the time to do it right.

Some factors you might include:

◆How much you feel you can afford to pay out of pocket (this might apply more in the case of a pet)

◆Whether you have the means at home to resolve this situation yourself

◆Whether you are as competent to deal with this situation yourself

- ◆ Whether this is a potentially life-threatening situation

- ◆ Whether your taking care of this situation will take longer than if you went to a doctor

- ◆ Whether going to a doctor would speed the recovery process and go easier on the patient

Once you have a complete list, you can dowse your question:

Considering the factors that matter the most to me, what is the overall level in effects of consulting a health care professional about this situation on a scale of +10 to -10, with positive numbers meaning good outcomes and 0 meaning no effect and negative meaning a bad result.

Then ask the question this way and compare the answers:

Considering the factors that matter most to me, what is the overall level in effects of NOT consulting a health care professional about this situation, but instead using methods known to or accessible by me, on a scale of +10 to -10, with positive numbers indicating a good outcome and 0 being no effect and negative numbers meaning a bad outcome.

Usually you will end up with 2 very different numbers. If one is positive and the other 0 or negative, go with the positive choice. If one is much more positive than the other, choose that. If they are very close, we would suggest looking at your list and seeing if you can think of any other factors that matter to you, add them in and re-dowse the questions.

If it appears no matter how you define it that either choice is ok, you can verify that by dowsing:

Does it make any difference in terms of outcome whether I consult a professional or deal with this situation myself?

If there is no real difference between each option, just go with whatever feels best to you.

Which Professional To Choose

If you don't have a regular doctor, or if you want to compare health care providers, because you aren't certain whom to consult, then dowsing can help you a lot.

Make a list of your reasons and goals for consulting a professional. Then make a list of the potential doctors and dowse this question:

Considering my specific health goals and desiring the best, quickest, most lasting positive outcome with minimal side effects, what is the overall level in effects on a scale of +10 to -10 of consulting Dr. _____ about this situation?

Get a number for each potential doctor by dowsing every name on your list. We recommend 8 or higher as the cutoff for taking action.

If none of the candidates is 8 or higher, then add to the list of doctors or go back and look at your specific health goals and see if maybe you should alter them. For example, if you have listed a goal of 'curing' a condition, then perhaps it cannot be cured as such. Maybe it can only be alleviated, and if so, none of the doctors would test 8 or higher, because a cure isn't possible.

Evaluating Results

As with all dowsing, you want to evaluate your results. It is the chief way of improving your dowsing. As with many health issues, you won't always have to dowse to evaluate your results. You may find yourself smiling at the doctor's amazing bedside manner and insights, and that will help you confirm you dowsed well.

On the other hand, if you are not happy with how things are going, if you don't feel you are getting the results you expected, then it is wise to go back and look at your list of goals and see if you feel the question was a good one. Or you may have been too attached to results, and your dowsing wasn't accurate for that reason.

Factors That Are Different With Children And Animals

Small children and pets cannot tell you what's wrong or what hurts. Dowsing is a very useful tool to have in your kit when working with small children or animals.

Often, handling a pet who feels bad only adds to the stress the animal is feeling. If you can use dowsing to get an overall picture of what's going on, that will limit the amount of time you have to spend handling the animal.

Often, when children are ill or coming down with something, they will have bad behavior that shows you something is out of balance. The same is true of animals, who often will exhibit negative behavior when they are in pain. An example is a cat peeing outside of the litter box when he has a bladder infection. Remember that bad behavior is usually a cry for help, so take the time to find out what's going on.

Permission Is Still Needed

When dowsing for a child or pet in your care, you are within our definition of ethical behavior. However, you still need to make sure you have their permission to dowse about them, or your work may be a waste of time.

For a child, ask if she minds you trying to help her feel better. You'll hardly ever get a 'no' answer. Explain only in as much detail as necessary to let the child know your intentions. Don't overwhelm or scare her into thinking she might get a shot, have to take pills or go to a doctor. If you sense reluctance, you may need to let the child talk about what's causing that feeling. Maybe a past experience being sick or going to a doctor left a bad impression.

For a pet, you can dowse if you have the animal's permission to help him get well. If you get a 'yes', which you will get most of the time, proceed. Of course, you can't talk it over with a pet if the pet says 'no'. It is rare that you won't get permission to help your pet. But it does happen.

What do you do if you can't get permission? Well, if you feel it is necessary to get help or do something to help your patient, do it. But be aware that a reluctant patient will usually not heal as quickly. It is important to acknowledge free will. There is no harm in continuing to offer assistance, and you have to follow your own judgment in health care situations. Don't ignore an obvious health issue just because the patient doesn't want treatment.

Being Detached Can Be Difficult…But It's Necessary

One of the most important reasons to dowse all the time is that it helps you develop a sense of detachment, and that is vital when dowsing about health issues. You can't expect to dowse well about important health issues if you don't dowse often. So practice your dowsing as much as possible, and cultivate a sense of curiosity about answers. It takes time, but it will increase your accuracy.

Teach Your Children To Dowse

Children take to dowsing particularly well. In fact, children are excellent at natural healing and energy techniques. We had a client who had a 3-yr-old who quickly learned to ask for EFT (Emotional Freedom Technique) when she was feeling out of balance.

If you teach your children to dowse, they will be able to participate in their healing process. It is terrific to get children empowered to use their intuitive sensing abilities and feel their health is something they can affect.

Make dowsing a game and fun for your children. Finding hidden objects is a good game. Having them dowse what color to wear for a certain outcome is fun. Slowly get them dowsing about things they have an opinion about, and teach them detachment, so they learn to listen to their intuition.

Euthanasia Of Pets

One of the most heart-wrenching situations for pet owners is when an older pet seems to have reached the end of her life. Often, the vet will say it's time to put the animal down. But some part of you isn't sure.

While it is often true that euthanasia is the appropriate choice, we have seen many situations where it was not. And by being able to use dowsing and follow their inner guidance, the pet owner had many more months, sometimes years, of quality time with their animal companion.

One example was my mother's German Shepherd, Sam. The vet told her the dog was old and had an inflammation of the spine which made it very hard for her to stand and walk, and it was not going to get better. He said to put the dog to sleep. My Mom came to me, and I did some dowsing and had her put the dog on a curcumin extract pill. The dog recovered the use of her hind end and lived happily for another 18 months, at which time she died of other causes.

We have had many pets in our lives, and on occasion, we have had to make a decision about euthanasia. We use dowsing to help us understand a number of factors that contribute to the decision. You can just dowse if it's appropriate based on your values and goals. Or you can go into more detail and find out what's going on with your beloved pet. Sometimes, more information is useful for making your decision.

We may sound like a broken record when we say you need to write all your goals down before dowsing, but once again, everyone has their own values about this subject. It isn't universal truth. Some people may have to consider whether the animal is incontinent, and they have no way of caring for an incontinent pet. Others may not feel they can leave a seriously ill or disabled animal alone all day while they go to work. Or some may have physical challenges that make it impossible to carry a large pet outside several times a day to go to the bathroom. Or they simply feel they don't have the resources to care for a seriously handicapped or ill elderly animal.

Some people don't care how much it costs; they will keep their pet with them as long as the pet is happy and wants to stay. Others may feel they have to consider the cost of pills and special feeding and such.

Make your list of what matters to you in this decision. It may include factors such as:

- How much time you have to care for a sick pet
- How strong you are
- How much money you have
- How much help you have for this project
- Whether the pet wants to stay here
- How much pain the pet is in
- If the pet can get well enough to enjoy life for a time
- Is the vet correct that the pet cannot improve and has no quality of life

Once you are very clear about the factors that matter for you, then you know what should contribute to a 'yes' answer and what would swing it to 'no' when you ask about euthanizing your pet.

Considering all the factors that matter to me, is it appropriate at this time to euthanize _____(name of pet)?

If you don't want to jump right to dowsing about that question, the following are dowsing questions you can ask that might give you information that could lead to other avenues you might want to pursue at this time:

- *On a scale of 0-10, with 0 being no pain and 10 being the most she can feel, what level of pain is my pet experiencing on average at this time?*
- *Does my pet feel she can recover and be healthy and feel good? (Sometimes pets are sick so long, they can't picture getting well, and that blocks them from healing).*

- *Does my pet want to move on/leave the planet at this time?*
- *Does my pet want to stay here with me? Is it only because she knows how bad I will feel without her? (Often they will choose to stay out of a sense of duty even when they are suffering).*
- *Is there any treatment, therapy or program that I can find and financially afford that would heal my pet and restore her to feeling comfortable?*

Depending on the answers you get, you might decide to pursue a second opinion on your pet's condition, or to do more research about options, the way my Mom did. However, you often discover that the pet is only hanging around because she knows how torn up you are about losing her. Pets are often more willing to move on than we are to let them go.

This is not always the case, however. Our dog India did not want to leave us, even when she had no quality of life. She was incontinent; couldn't eat or drink without vomiting; was in pain; couldn't walk. And still, she did not want to leave us.

We worked on ourselves, thinking it was us keeping her here, but it turned out she just didn't want to go. We told her she could come back to us as another pet in the future if she wanted to. It was hard to euthanize her, knowing she did not want to go, but it was very helpful being able to dowse in detail, and we felt we did the right thing at the right time. And in the end, that is really what you need and want most. You just want to do the best you can by your beloved pet.

Long Term Level In Effects Of What's Going On

One of the biggest gifts we can share with you about health in general is to help you see symptoms in a new way. Just because something is painful does not mean it is bad. It just means things are a bit chaotic or out of balance.

Even though you know this is true, you do not tend to apply that knowledge in health situations. If you hurt, you think something is wrong. Yet, if you just began a fitness program, don't your muscles usually cry out in pain the next day? Does that mean you need a doctor? No, of course not. You know better.

So why when you get an unexplained pain do you imagine some terrible health problem? Probably because pain is generally regarded as negative. But pain is just a symptom of an imbalance. It may be a sign of disease, or it might actually be something that leads to a positive outcome, like sore muscles after a workout.

You can dowse about any symptom you have, whether it is pain or discomfort or a rash. Here's the question we use:

On a scale of +10 to -10, where a positive number means an overall positive outcome, what is the long term level in effects on my health and well-being of the process that includes _____ (the current symptom)?

When The Answer Is Negative...

A negative number means that the symptom is part of a process that has an overall negative impact on your long term health. The bigger the number, the more serious it is.

A negative number might indicate a disease process, like a virus or bacterial infection. It might represent food poisoning or other toxicity. It could indicate a parasitic overgrowth/infection.

If you get a negative number, then you will want to treat the cause of the problem so you can resolve the symptoms and the process. You can dowse to see what therapy or remedy will best resolve the cause.

When It's Positive...

If on the other hand, the answer is a positive number, then, like sore muscles after a workout, your symptoms are a sign of a process that has a long term positive overall effect on your health. The bigger the number, the more positive it is.

Positive processes can be things like a detox, a healing crisis or a transformative process of some type.

If you get a positive number, you want to support the process and make it as comfortable as possible without stopping it. You can dowse to see what therapy or remedy will best support the process and allow it to bring positive results to you, while minimizing discomfort.

Finding The Cause

In most cases, if you can dowse the best way to resolve or support the process, it really doesn't matter that much what the original cause is. However, sometimes it can be useful or even important to know the cause. Chart or list dowsing is a good way to determine causes. Always be sure 'other' is an option, as no list is complete.

A cause could be physical, like an infection or trauma. Or it could be energetic, like a chakra link or aura damage. There are so many possible causes, it is beyond the scope of this book to list them all. You can make a list of those you are familiar with and dowse it.

Once you discover the cause, you can dowse what the best therapy or remedy to resolve it will be. Remember to only apply things that rank 8 or higher on a scale of 10, for best results.

All The Questions

On a scale of +10 to -10, with 0 being average for my gender, age and culture, what is my overall physical health at this time?

On a scale of +10 to -10, with 0 being average for my gender, age and culture, what is the overall physical health of my _____ System at this time?

On a scale of +10 to -10, with 0 being average for my gender, age and culture, what is the overall physical health of my _____ at this time?

On a scale of 0 to 10, with 0 being none and 10 being the worst/most it could be, what is the level/degree of physical_____ in my physical body at this time?

Are there any _____ at this time in my aura that are having a significant effect on the health and well-being of my aura?

On a scale of 0 to 100%, with 100% being the best and most optimal functioning, what is the value of my EM Field as an average over the last 7 days?

Is red/blue/purple/silver/gold the best color for me to use to repair, restore and strengthen my EM Field at this time?

Will supplementation by any of these products be an 8 or higher on a scale of 10 (with 10 being the most helpful) for creating excellent immune balance, good energy levels and excellent physical function for my body at this time when taken as directed?

Are any of these products an 8 or higher on a scale of 10 for reaching my overall health goals at this time when taken as directed?

How long would it be best for me to take this supplement to reach my health goals: More than 30 days? More than 60 days? More than 90 days?

How many bottles of this supplement taken at the suggested dosage will be required for me to reach my health goals? 1? 2? 3?

What is the overall effectiveness of my entire program of supplements for my health goals at this time if I include this new product?

How allergic/sensitive am I to _____ on a scale of 0 to 10, with 0 being not allergic at all and 10 being the most allergic I could be?

How effective on a scale of 0-10 would the _____ diet be for achieving my health and fitness goals at this time?

What would be the overall Level in Effects of my following the _____ diet on my health and fitness goals on a scale of +10 to -10?

How long will I need to be on the _____ diet to achieve my goal of losing ten pounds? More than one month? More than two? Etc.

What is the overall level in effects for me of participating in _____ as a means of reaching my fitness goals on a scale of +10 to -10, with 0 having no effect and positive numbers having increasingly positive effects?

How long would I need to participate in _____ to reach my stated fitness goals? More than one month? More than two? Etc.

On a scale of +10 to -10, with 0 being neutral and positive numbers meaning I would enjoy success and negative numbers meaning I would dislike it/not get results, what is the value of participating in _____ for me at this time for my fitness goals and enjoyment?

Considering all my goals and desiring a minimum of negative side effects, what is the overall level in effects of using _____ (fill in the blank with a therapy) on a scale of +10 to -10 at this time as directed for my specific health goals (as listed), with a positive number meaning it will enhance health and a negative number meaning it will detract from health.

Considering my specific health goals, what is the best length of time for me to use this therapy to restore balance and health and resolve the cause of my physical symptoms? More than one week? More than one month? Etc.

Considering the factors that matter the most to me, what is the overall level in effects of consulting a health care professional about this situation on a scale of +10 to -10, with positive numbers meaning good outcomes and 0 meaning no effect.

Considering the factors that matter most to me, what is the overall level in effects of NOT consulting a health care professional about this situation, but instead using methods known to or accessible by me, on a scale of +10 to -10, with positive numbers indicating a good outcome and 0 being no effect and negative numbers meaning a bad outcome.

Considering my specific health goals and desiring the best, quickest, most lasting positive outcome with minimal side effects, what is the overall level in effects on a scale of +10 to -10 of consulting Dr. _____ about this situation?

Considering all the factors that matter to me, is it appropriate at this time to euthanize _____ (name of pet)?

- On a scale of 0-10, with 0 being no pain and 10 being the most she can feel, what level of pain is my pet experiencing on average at this time?

- Does my pet feel she can recover and be healthy and feel good? (Sometimes pets are sick so long, they can't picture getting well, and that blocks them from healing).

- Does my pet want to move on/leave the planet at this time?

- Does my pet want to stay here with me? Is it only because she knows how bad I will feel without her? (Often they will choose to stay out of a sense of duty).

- Is there any treatment, therapy or program that I can find and afford to apply financially that would heal my pet and restore her to feeling comfortable?

On a scale of +10 to -10, where a positive number means an overall positive outcome, what is the long term level in effects on my health and well-being of the process that includes _____(the current symptom)?

∽

Dowsing Deeper...

The questions in this book have helped us transform our lives; save lots of money; become healthier and more successful. But can you improve on them? Of course you can!

Each person is an individual. You have your own point of view made up of your values, beliefs and how you define and rate things in terms of your preferences.

Your dowsing question will be affected by all these things. A question asked using Maggie Percy's definitions of terms and her goals will be a good question for her, but it may or may not be a perfect question for you.

The best way to be sure to get dowsing answers that work for you is to create your own questions. This section will guide you in how to do that. It's only for serious dowsers who really want to improve their accuracy, because they intend to use dowsing to make their life better, or to help others.

We believe that learning to ask good dowsing questions not only improves your dowsing; it makes you think about your beliefs, values and preferences, and that causes you to live more consciously, to question things and to actively choose to create the life you want.

What Are Your Goals?

Not everyone has the exact same goals. Some people don't even really HAVE goals. So the first thing to do is to know your goals and to think about them in detail, so that when you create a dowsing question, you have a clear purpose for asking it, and you are aiming to achieve your goals.

Good goals are detailed and personal. You can ask what is healthy for you, or what will make you healthier, but what do you mean by that? Do you want to eliminate pain? Do you want to be able to have lots of energy? Do you want to run a marathon easily?

Think about the subject you are dowsing about, and ask yourself exactly what you hope to achieve by using a therapy, taking a supplement or consulting a doctor. What is the positive outcome you wish to create?

List the things that you consider important factors in your dowsing answer. For example, some people feel they can't spend more than a certain amount of money. If that is true for you, put it clearly in your list. You may really care about consulting a professional who will want your participation, rather than pushing you around. If so, put that on the list.

What Do Your Words Mean?

Too often, you use words that you haven't clearly defined. You may think you know what they mean, but you don't. If you use vague, undefined terms, your answer won't necessarily be accurate for you.

We spoke earlier of not using vague terms like "good", "healthy", "highest and greatest good". These words and phrase have vague meanings, or none at all. Don't use them.

Instead, think about words that mean something specific to you and relate to your goals. "Having enough energy to do whatever I feel like", "feeling physically good and comfortable", "improving my memory significantly" are examples of specific terms and phrases.

People use poor words when they are lazy, or if they lack confidence or just are living unconsciously. Dowsing will help you question your values and get you to act more consciously, which will help you manifest positive outcomes.

Don't use other people's definitions of terms unless you are sure you agree with them.

Include All The Parts Of A Good Question

Poor questions often are poor because they lack an important element. A good question should include how, what, where, when, who and why.

Time is a critical aspect that is often overlooked. "At this time" is a good phrase to add to any question when you are testing something for right now.

Indicate whom you are dowsing the therapy/supplement/remedy for.

Include when you intend to apply what you are dowsing about, and for how long.

Add in as appropriate how often or what dosage you will be using.

Be sure to include why you are asking the question; what is the goal.

A good dowsing question is usually long and detailed.

Check Your Answers

As often as possible, write down your question and your answer, and then after an appropriate time, check your answer for accuracy.

Sometimes the answer is accurate, but you left out an important part, so it appears to be wrong. Here's an example: Maggie dowsed that she would be given approval for a home loan modification. She had gone through a laborious process with Bank of America, and it dowsed that a home loan modification would be approved.

But she left something out. She left out 'when'. Because she was caught up in the filing of paperwork and was very focused on the present process, it didn't occur to her to add a time.

BAC rejected the application after 18 months of haggling. Maggie couldn't believe her dowsing, which had felt so accurate, was wrong, but she had to accept facts.

Then, 3 years later, the mortgage was sold to another company, who approached Maggie about applying for a home loan modification. Not being keen on going through 18 months of trouble, she was hesitant, but did it anyway. Within 3 months, approval came through, and the modification was granted.

Maggie's dowsing was right, but she only found that out later. Look at your question. If it appears wrong, ask yourself if you included ALL the aspects of a good question. Ask yourself how you could change the question and have it be correct. If Maggie had done that exercise, she might have realized that maybe the answer WAS correct, but not for that case.

Making mistakes is a great way to improve your dowsing if you take the time to check your answers and find ways to improve how you ask questions. Don't be upset if you make a mistake…learn from it!

Study Your Subject

If you want to be a good health dowser, study about the physical body, how it works and learn about organs, systems and ailments. Read about allergies and different diets. Get some good books with illustrations of anatomy. An anatomy coloring book can be quite useful. Find a health guru who resonates with you and subscribe to her blog. Read books related to physical health. The more you know, the better your questions will be. You don't have to have 2 Biology degrees like Maggie, but it can be a real blessing.

14

RESOURCES

Books

Good Books On Physical & Energetic Health

There are too many great books to list here, but a few that have been instrumental in my healing journey are mentioned below.

Dr. F. Batmanghelidj's book *Your Body's Many Cries For Water* came out in 1995, which is about the time I bought and read it for the first time. It opened my eyes to the value of staying fully hydrated, but it wasn't until I read it a second time in 2017, after years of other reading, that I gleaned even more from the book. The early edition was poorly edited, but there is a newer version that may have been cleaned up and made easier to understand. Regardless, this book is worth a read, especially if it motivates you to quit drinking 'bad' stuff and drink more pure water.

Vitamin K2 and the Calcium Paradox: How A Little-Known Vitamin Could Save Your Life by Kate Rheaume-Bleue was published in 2013, and I didn't run across it until early 2018, but it has literally changed my life. I recommend it to everyone. Read it twice. Read it three times. A compelling, well-written and documented work.

Robb Wolf's book, *The Paleo Solution: The Original Human Diet* came out in 2011, and I stumbled across it in 2012, and we went paleo immediately, because he uses evolutionary biology and our physiology to prove paleo is a natural diet for us. No diet is perfect for everyone, but we maintain that if you live 'naturally', you will be more healthy. Be aware that applying paleo is the tricky bit, as you shouldn't overdo meat when you remove grains from your diet. You must still maintain a 'natural' balance of food types, and meat was never a huge part of the human diet.

Hands of Light by Barbara Brennan is chock full of useful information on energy healing techniques and includes an extensive section on the use of a pendulum to show the function of your chakras. This classic can be found cheap secondhand, and it is well worth reading and keeping for reference.

The Biology Of Belief by Bruce Lipton goes into some detail about how beliefs affect your biology. I found it a slightly disappointing read, but there are some gems, especially if this topic is new for you.

You Are The Placebo by Joe Dispenza is another book that covers how what you believe and think affects your physical reality. He discusses real studies that support his theories and makes a good case for taking charge of what you think and creating your own health.

Books That Interpret Energetic Causes Of Symptoms

Messages From The Body: Their Psychological Meaning by Michael J. Lincoln, Ph.D. This is our go-to book, but it's expensive to buy new. It is the most comprehensive book we have found, and we use it a lot. If you intend to do serious self-work, this is a must-have book.

You Can Heal Your Life by Louise Hay is a good introductory book on this topic.

Feelings Buried Alive Never Die by Karol Truman is on the same level as Louise Hay's, a very good introductory book.

The Body Is The Barometer Of The Soul by Annette Noontil has a little more detail than Louise Hay's book.

Your Body's Telling You: "Love Yourself!" by Lise Bourbeau is another good book on this topic.

The Busy Person's Guides & Dowsing Books

Our series *The Busy Person's Guides* help you get competent quickly on subjects like energy clearing, space clearing, ghosts, curses and aliens, and more.

Our course-in-a-book, *Learn Dowsing: Your Natural Psychic Power*, is available in all formats at all online retailers. If you want to learn how to dowse, we suggest you get that book.

Good Resources For Understanding Energy, Intention & Natural Health

THE INTERNET IS an infinite resource of great information on these subjects, but here are a couple of starting places:

The Weston A. Price Foundation, https://www.westonaprice.org/, is a great source for information about natural diet and health. I get my fat-soluble vitamin supplement (fermented cod liver oil and butter oil) via a company recommended on their site. Dr. Weston A. Price was the dentist who decades ago did a comprehensive study that showed modern diet was the cause of many dental issues as well as health problems, and he identified what was missing and created a solution with his supplement. His goal was to in essence make it unnecessary to go to your dentist very often as well as to experience excellent health.

The Intention Experiment by Lynne McTaggart is a landmark book that looks at scientific studies that prove beyond a doubt that intention works, although the proof always revolves around group intention.

But it is an excellent starting point for convincing yourself of the power of intention and to think about applications.

The Hidden Messages In Water by Masaru Emoto is another book that shows scientifically that intention works. Dr. Emoto worked mainly with how water changes when subjected to intention, and considering our bodies are mostly water, this is a very foundational work.

The Law Of Attraction is a powerful way to look at your ability to manifest consciously. While it is not easy to master the LOA, we believe it is true and does work. Approach the LOA as you do dowsing. Study, practice and read about it. There are books, events and a free daily quote here: https://www.abraham-hicks.com/

PLEASE LEAVE A REVIEW

We love helping people learn about dowsing. If you enjoyed this book and learned from it, please leave a review wherever you bought it to help other dowsers decide if it will be a good investment for them. Thanks for your support!

ABOUT THE AUTHORS

Maggie and Nigel Percy met online in 2000 through their mutual love of dowsing. They spent the next 20+ years serving a global clientele with dowsing and energy clearing methods. During that time, they presented at many conferences, created the online Dowsing World Summit and gave free dowsing training through videos and articles on their websites.

They've written over 20 books on dowsing and metaphysical topics and have published fiction using the pen names Maggie McPhee and Andrew Elgin. To see all their books, visit your favorite online retailer.

www.ingramcontent.com/pod-product-compliance
Lightning Source LLC
Chambersburg PA
CBHW071652090426
42738CB00009B/1502